Could It Be?

Biblical Gems from the Garbage Dump

Joseph C. Way, BA, BD, MDiv

ISBN 978-1-961358-10-2 (paperback)
ISBN 978-1-961358-11-9 (digital)

Could It Be?

Biblical Gems from the Garbage Dump

BY

JOSEPH C. WAY
BA, BD, MDiv

Contents

Could It Be?

Biblical Gems from the Garbage Dump

BY

JOSEPH C. WAY
BA, BD, MDiv

DEDICATION

To my children, William and Wanda, who delight me
with their eagerness and ability to appropriately ask,
"Could it be?"

JOSEPH C. WAY

INTRODUCTION

I delight in stirring the status quo. That is one purpose for this book! My profession as a clergyman, chaplain, counselor, teacher and therapist required that from me and also offered extensive opportunities for it. Without someone repeatedly stirring, our life becomes stale and static. The stirring process is sometimes initiated and continued by and for ourselves. Most often, another initiates it. We may join in or opt out. Stirring the status quo is absolutely essential for intellectual and spiritual growth.

This new descriptive insight into myself came as I pondered the content of this book. I began seriously stirring the status quo as a teenager. I am the fifth of seven siblings, the only one who planned and planted my own crops, owned livestock, provided financial support for myself while in high school and living with my parents. Furthermore, I was their first offspring to attend college, the only one who completed graduate school, and the only one who became a minister.

My most painful experiences during forty-two years of pastoral ministry came as a direct result of attempting to stir the status quo. Every congregational confrontation and every request for my removal as its pastor came from that. A Mississippi Methodist bishop and his helpers refused to assign me as the pastor of a church because I, along with others, stirred the status quo on integration. The few skirmishes I had while serving as an Air Force chaplain, therapist and counselor were directly related to my desire to change something for the betterment of others.

My most rewarding experiences also came as a result of stirring the status quo. Those adult responsibilities as a teenager taught me lessons unavailable elsewhere. Successfully working my way through high school, college and graduate school, without any lingering debt, was an education in itself. Many parishioners in little country churches were excited over my new insights into scripture and asked for more.

Some of my dearest friends and life-changing experiences came out of the struggles over integration in Mississippi. While serving as the associate pastor of a large down-town church in Jackson from June 1963 to June 1964, I received threats on my life, deliberate harassment from members of the congregation and false publicity in the newspaper. However, that was perhaps the most effective and most memorable year in my ministry.

During my military and V. A. chaplaincy, I developed a new approach for dealing with addiction which was affirmed by more than one long time addict who asked, "Where have you been all my life?"
These momentous experiences, for me and perhaps others, would not have occurred had I not stirred the status quo.

After over seventy years of living, I realize that a productive and meaningful life is not "like a box of chocolate." It is much more like making cakes. An avid cake maker is never fully satisfied with the most recent cake but learns from it and incorporates that learning experience into the next cake. Their cake making is always in process, perhaps reasonably well pleased with the last one but seeking to be different and better with the next. They stir not only the batter but also the status quo, and discover wonderful new cakes.

A healthy and wholesome life is always in process, lacking final form and finish. Like making cakes, each human life starts with very similar ingredients into which someone stirs specific elements that make it individually special and hopefully better. If no new or different ingredients are ever added, cakes soon become commonplace, predictable and possibly unwanted. So it is with life. If we want our life to be exciting, enriching and expanding, we must deliberately stir well chosen and distinctive ingredients into it. I trust this book provides those ingredients.

Stirring life's status quo demands examination of ideas, customs and behavior most often taken for granted. Stirring occurs at a conscious and unconscious level. It is most helpful when purposefully and diligently done.

The only road leading to intellectual and spiritual growth runs through the crowded and musty city of "Old Ideas" and winds through the treacherous valley of "New Possibilities." Refusal to travel that road is a refusal to stir or be stirred. Refusal to stir or be stirred signifies a sad situation almost synonymous with death. In that state of existence, breathing continues but there is little life left.

Stirring the status quo is often done with a loud voice speaking about an emotional issue. There are other and more effective ways to stir. It is normally done on behalf of some specific concern and in allegiance to what is commonly called a higher cause. Anyone who seeks to be genuinely Christian must always be aware of the cause for which and the method by which they stir. For them, stirring the status quo should be done only when it is in keeping with Christian principles and is the appropriate thing to do, not because one wishes to cause trouble or receive recognition at any cost.

This book is another attempt to stir the status quo, first for myself and then hopefully for others. If I correctly understand the conditions of our modern day, we desperately need additional stirring with some new and some tried and true ingredients included in the mix. I repeatedly hear and see evidence of the urgency for deliberate and serious stirring.

An illustration of our present need is the simple fact that Judeo-Christian signs, symbols and sayings are denied public display. Devout Christians crave new insights at the cutting edge of religious faith and life but are seldom introduced to them within their religious community. Some who once sought to be genuinely religious gave up on the process, either because they did not understand the rigid and ridiculous requirements or they could not stand those who claimed to have all the exact answers. Uninformed and unchallenged church members drifted beyond the church's influence because they were fed nothing more than mealy-mouthed mush.

Exuberant and erroneous interpretations of theological issues and scriptural passages disturbed and divided church members. Those senseless interpretations and irrational ideas caused too many potential believers to relegate them to the religious garbage dump.

Many who consider themselves a part of the Christian community profess an easy and simplistic religion that makes little or no demands for Christ-like living. Overly opinionated and under educated persons become self-appointed gurus demanding unquestioned allegiance.

Many who once stood outside the church and consider coming in chose to turn aside because the religious community offered nothing as good as, and certainly no better than, what they already had.
Stirring is essential because many of us were taught, at church and at home, that many beloved and well-known narratives were each a one-time special event for special people in a special situation. Numerous narratives were presented as events over which no ordinary person had control, could duplicate or experience.

We were also taught that all biblical directives must be followed, regardless of the difficulty. Anyone who sought to interpret them from a more human perspective was chastised for being frivolous and irreligious, with threats of eternal punishment for making them "too human."

As a result of such teachings, some of us concluded God acts only in supernatural ways, only for specifically chosen people, and only reveals himself in extraordinary people, things and events. If that is true, there is little reason to expect God's action in or around us. We also found it impossible to fulfill the biblical admonitions and were firmly chastised for our failure. Therefore, many of us secretly questioned our place in God's great design and the significance of these fervently repeated stories and admonitions.

Unless we were very unusual, we eventually accused God of playing favorites, considered ourselves unworthy and unlikely recipients for a similar experience, seriously questioned the authenticity of the stories, disregarded the admonitions and doubted their relevance to us. By default, these stories and admonitions became little more than religious garbage. However, we were still uneasy about our decision, unhappy with our conclusion and unsatisfied with our religion.

If many of these stories reflect normal and repeatable events that happened to ordinary people, then we may rightfully conclude that similar experiences can happen to us. We need not sit and halfheartedly wait for God to blast us with some magical, mystical and momentous event. Instead, we seriously ponder God's repeated miracles in common events and earthly things, seeking to discover something we had not seen before. We now consciously seek what God has to say to us, to discover how we may move all our actions and thoughts closer to divine truth and reality.

We facilitate the stirring process by simply changing the names and locations for many of these narratives and each becomes our story, reflecting our personal experience of agony and ecstasy. They are no longer just the story of some long ago biblical character but they are now the human story, thus our story and our experience. They are now "MY STORY." Adherence to an admonition is for MY edification. Daily life is now more than just ho-hum human experiences because it is connected to, in the midst of and a unique part of God's eternal and present activity to revel himself.

For all those reasons, and more, sensible and serious persons must stir the present religious status quo before it is too late. That is a basic reason for writing this book and for its format. My ability to effectively and properly stir may be questioned. Having previously experienced some success in stirring, I have a strong desire to stir again. I also invite you to join me in this challenging and dangerous endeavor.

If we properly and successfully stir, we must do it in keeping with the love and spirit of Christ.

Could it be that the appropriate place to stir is a new examination and interpretation of seriously misunderstood biblical passages? This book focuses on selected biblical passages, many of which have been previously denigrated or disregarded by various people, some who want nothing to do with a religious community and some who claim to be genuinely Christian. Formulating and recording my own thoughts provided an opportunity to stir my own status quo in response to scripture. I trust this book will serve a similar purpose for all who read it.

I composed the following poem to paraphrase this introduction and this book:

GOD'S INCLUSIVENESS

We can read old Bible stories In ways that make
them very new, If we are mindful how God acts,
And observe the human acts too.

What we tend to call a miracle, And declare it was
very odd, When truly understood by us, Was a
normal action for God.

God's gracious acts on behalf of
People who lived in days of yore, Were not reserved
only for them, And are offered now as before.

Since God's actions for them and us Are similar, if
not the same,

These stories are new to us when, For theirs,
we substitute our name.

CHAPTER ONE
The Blazing Bush
Exodus 3:1-6

1: Now Moses was keeping the flock of his father-in-law, Jethro, the priest of Mid'ian; and he led his flock to the west side of the wilderness, and came to Horeb, the mountain of God.

2: And the angel of the LORD appeared to him in a flame of fire out of the midst of a bush; and he looked, and lo, the bush was burning, yet it was not consumed.

3: And Moses said, "I will turn aside and see this great sight, why the bush is not burnt."

4: When the LORD saw that he turned aside to see, God called to him out of the bush, "Moses, Moses!" And he said, "Here am I."

5: Then he said, "Do not come near; put off your shoes from your feet, for the place on which you are standing is holy ground."

6: And he said, "I am the God of your father, the God of Abraham, the God of Isaac, and the God of Jacob." And Moses hid his face, for he was afraid to look at God.

The opening verses of the third chapter of Exodus present the familiar story of Moses and a blazing bush that was not consumed. He was working as a common shepherd, tending the flock of his father-in-law, Jethro. As was customary for shepherds, Moses daily traveled a great distance to find adequate grazing for the flock under his care.

By accident, deliberate choice or divine intervention, Moses came to Mt. Horeb, called "The Mountain of God."

We are not sure Moses knew where he was or if the location was identified later. If he knew where he was, the sacred place had some significance to Moses. We have no way of knowing what went through his mind as he came to and spent some time on that spot. If he recognized he was on "The Mountain of God," it seems safe to assume that he was more attuned to thoughts about God.

If Moses had previously contemplated the mystery and majesty of God or the possibility of becoming God's special servant, we have no indication of it. Long and lonesome days spent in desolate places talking only to smelly sheep and himself may have caused him to think about another occupation and eventually speak to God about it. In one way or another, previous experiences and present circumstances may have facilitated his thoughts and response. Whatever the situation or condition, the blazing bush was no ordinary experience for Moses because he turned his full attention from the flock to it.

Following the encounter with God through a flaming bush that was not consumed, Moses was a different man. The scripture uses human words in a feeble attempt to describe and explain what Moses saw and his transformation that followed. Then and now, no one can adequately or completely convey to another the depth or meaning in a transforming experience. We are limited by the common words and experiences known to each person. At the end of this story, we are left with our own imagination and experiences to interpret its full meaning to Moses.

Few, if any, of us have ever actually heard the voice of God calling from a blazing bush that was or was not consumed. Few people ever make that claim. Those who do are usually labeled schizophrenic and are frequently found in a mental hospital. Therefore, we tend to write off this story as ancient, unrealistic and basically irrelevant to any of us because it happened to a special person for a special purpose in a special way, none of which we understand.

We tend to dismiss it as a human interest story that provides a bit of data on a biblical hero, imagined or real, but one that has nothing to do with us in the here and now.

Could it be that there is another way to interpret this story, one that makes it as relevant as the air we breathe and as modern as the latest fashions from Vogue? Could it be that God repeatedly acts in a similar way but we fail to see "the blazing bush?" Perhaps God performed similar miracles millions of times but no one ever noticed? Could it be that God regularly repeats his ancient miracles but we have become so accustomed to them that we no longer call them miracles and no longer look or listen for his message?

Such ancient miracles occur daily, if only we were capable of seeing them. While serving as an Air Force chaplain in the Philippines, I repeatedly saw a blazing bush (actually a tree) that was not consumed. The natives call it "The Flame Tree." At certain times of the year, its foliage is bright reddish orange. When you look at it from a distance, with a gently breeze blowing, the tree literally appears to be burning. The gentle movement of its abundant leaves so realistically imitates active flames that you think the foliage should be consumed…. but it isn't! The first time I saw that tree, like Moses, I knew I must turn aside to see it.

Poinsettias grow into medium size trees on the Island of Crete because there is no frost in many areas. In full color, a poinsettia tree closely resembles a flame tree and could be the catalyst for an unusual experience the first time someone sees it. It also resembles a burning bush that is not consumed.

Could this story about Moses be an actual account of the first time he saw a flame tree, or poinsettia, or something similar, and the transforming religious experience it produced? If he had no prior knowledge of the tree's existence, he automatically described the new experience in terms with which he was familiar.

From his previous experiences, it looked just like a burning bush but it was not consumed, as every other burning thing he had seen. It did not behave as he expected. If from nothing more than curiosity, he felt compelled to examine it more closely. Having discovered its true nature, Moses recognized it as God's special handiwork and it led to a deep religious experience that forever changed Moses.

That tree was no new miracle for God. He had annually performed it for years. It was a miracle to Moses. From the story, we know it was the first time Moses had seen such a sight. We know flame trees and poinsettias exist and there is no logical reason to doubt they, or something similar, existed where Moses was.

Could it be that the ears of Moses did not actually hear the voice of God? Perhaps Moses was deeply moved by the magnificent experience that may have lasted for hours or days! He was convinced beyond any doubt that God had a message for him. How was he to describe that experience? He could not. The best he could do was to use words that could not fully explain or describe.

Perhaps he punctuated the forcefulness of the experience by saying, "The message was so plain it was as if the voice of God actually spoke it in my ear." What could he say other than "I heard the voice of God?" He "heard" it in the core of his being, not in his ear. If that is how it happened, it is no less a miracle. We can identify with that because that is how it happens to us, if it happens.

Sometime during this transforming experience, Moses reportedly removed his shoes because he realized he stood on holy ground. Most of us have assumed the "holy ground" on which he stood refers to Mt. Horeb or "The Mountain of God." Could it be that we have missed the point again? Perhaps genuine "holy ground" is not necessarily a particular place so labeled by another but is hallowed by the transforming experience one has on that spot.

That spot on which Moses stood was his private holy ground because he had experienced God there as never before. His transforming experience with God, not the physical location, made it holy for him, even if for no other person. After that, he removed his shoes as a sign of respect and reverence. Apparently, he did not consider that particular spot holy ground prior to his experience there.

This interpretation makes good sense and deserves serious consideration because it duplicates common human experiences. We can identify with it because most of us have a particular spot where we experienced God as never before. Our personal holy ground may be the kneeling rail at a country church or an elaborate cathedral, a church camp by the lake or a silent moment alone with God. No matter where it is or what others call it, it is "holy ground" for us.

This interpretation does not deny the mighty power of God. No one else can make a flame tree or a poinsettia. God still makes both of them! God did not necessarily formulate a new miracle for the benefit of Moses. The new miracle was that God got the attention of Moses through an ordinary thing! The natural ground on which Moses stood remained the same but he was forever partial to that place where he experienced deep awe and reverence.

If this is what happened with Moses, then we too have stood on potential holy ground. "Flame trees" of one sort or another are all around us and they have been there all the time. God does not necessarily need to change his laws to perform a new miracle on our behalf. He can repeat the old ones because we are often unaware of his action unless or until something happens to open our eyes to God's activity and presence. Having experienced God in a special way at a youth camp, church altar, some cataclysmic occurrence, etc., that spot will always be holy ground for us and that experience will always be our "flame tree." This interpretation changes nothing in the narrative. It does change our approach to it and provides a way for us to make it relevant to our own life. Through this approach we personally identify with Moses because the story depicts our own religious experiences.

We also describe them as "hearing the voice of God" because we are sure God conveyed a message to us, even though it was not audible.

From this perspective, this story is no longer just an ancient narrative about a special person but is a story of God's action for and about us, set in the midst of our regular world. It places the story where we live. It is now my story. Since it is my story, I can no longer avoid it or relegate it to the distant past. For much too long, that ploy kept it from demanding anything from me. This ancient and modern story reflects present-day judgment, hope and challenge. Perhaps we should have left it as ancient history! It pronounces judgment on us for the many times we stood in the presence of a "blazing bush," a potential revelation of God, and did not notice it. We mistakenly called it a common occurrence, were more interested in other matters, did not have time to be bothered, or didn't want to pull off our shoes. Our old deep seated religious ideas kept us from expecting or finding anything other than the ordinary. God was there and we never noticed!

Ancient and regularly repeated miracles of God confront us at every turn. Our failure to see or hear is not God's fault because he silently screams in the common things of life. God is and has always been in the midst of them but we fail to notice unless and until something special happens to us. This is a refreshing story of hope. If God used something like an ordinary flame tree or poinsettia to convey a vital message to Moses, then there is hope that some ordinary thing will clearly convey God's message to us. We may now believe that the ancient ways of God are operative in our world. God does not act only for special peoplei n special ways during special times. He constantly acts where we are. What we have often called ordinary is no longer just ordinary. The simple things in our life are often resplendent with glorious possibilities available to those who can see them. If we fail to find transforming experiences, it is not God's fault but our own weakness. Since God is presently working in our every day world and since he wants us to recognize his handiwork, there is hope for everyone.

Seen from this new approach, this story challenges us to look for "blazing bushes that are not consumed," to look at normal events and things from a different perspective. Without doubt, they exist all around us, possibly just beyond our front door. I saw another one on the steep slopes of northern Alaska where flowers are so small they are almost invisible to the naked eye. When magnified, they are as intricate and multi-colored as their larger cousins. Even though they are very tiny, their abundance enables them to color the mountainside. If you ever see them, please pull off your shoes! They are holy ground for me.

Several years ago, if not now, you could periodically drive a short distance west of Phoenix, Arizona and find acres and acres of different colored roses in full bloom. Their pungent and pleasant flagrancy filled the air long before they became visible to the traveler. They were ablaze with rich color but they were not consumed. Such beauty is "holy ground." Who has not witnessed a glorious sunrise on a cool autumn morning that looks as if the eastern sky is on fire? Most of us have marveled at an indescribable sunset whose flaming spectacle fills the western horizon, but it was not consumed.

All who label this story of Moses as a "one time event for a special person in a special place" apparently do not understand the activity of God, the mystery and miracles in common occurrences, and the transforming experience in such a discovery. Sunsets, roses and similar things are not quite the same as flame trees, and poinsettias but are they terribly different? I know of no person who can make a sunset, a rose, a poinsettia or a flame tree. God apparently has no trouble repeating these and numerous other miracles.

Behind each one God speaks his truth to all who will hear. Like Moses, we are able to find our "blazing bush" with a message from God in some new experience and in what we have often called common. Such experiences must have been in the mind of Elizabeth Barrett Browning when she reportedly said, "…every common bush afire with God." The "blazing bush" continues to burn and it is not consumed! Have you seen it?

CHAPTER TWO
Bothersome Brothers
Genesis 25:21-34

21: And Isaac prayed to the LORD for his wife, because she was barren; and the LORD granted his prayer, and Rebekah his wife conceived.

22: The children struggled together within her; and she said, "If it is thus, why do I live?" So she went to inquire of the LORD.

23: And the LORD said to her, "Two nations are in your womb, and two peoples, born of you, shall be divided; the one shall be stronger than the other, the elder shall serve the younger."

24: When her days to be delivered were fulfilled, behold, there were twins in her womb.

25: The first came forth red, all his body like a hairy mantle; so they called his name Esau.

26: Afterward his brother came forth, and his hand had taken hold of Esau's heel; so his name was called Jacob. Isaac was sixty years old when she bore them.

27: When the boys grew up, Esau was a skilful hunter, a man of the field, while Jacob was a quiet man, dwelling in tents.

28: Isaac loved Esau, because he ate of his game; but Rebekah loved Jacob.

29: Once when Jacob was boiling pottage, Esau came in from the field, and he was famished.

30: And Esau said to Jacob, "Let me eat some of that red pottage, for I am famished!" (Therefore, his name was called Edom.

31: Jacob said, "First sell me your birthright."

32: Esau said, "I am about to die; of what use is a birthright to me?"

33: Jacob said, "Swear to me first." So he swore to him, and sold his birthright to Jacob.

34: Then Jacob gave Esau bread and pottage of lentils, and he ate and drank, and rose and went his way. Thus Esau despised his birthright.

The intriguing story of Jacob and Esau is actually a supporting chapter in the long saga about Abraham and/or Israel. At the first reading of the above passage, it appears to be a straightforward and simple story about a strange and dysfunctional family. Isaac married Rebekah when he was forty years old. He was approaching sixty years of age but had fathered no child. He and his wife prayed to God who heard their prayer and gave them twin sons. Old Isaac may have had snow on the roof but undoubtedly there was some fire in his boiler!

   As a prelude to what followed, Jacob and Esau fought with each other while in their mother's womb. The inner conflict greatly disturbed Rebekah and she sought divine guidance on what she should do. Esau was born first but Jacob came from the womb holding the heel of his brother. The fraternal, certainly not identical, twins had little in common except their gender and genes. Their looks, personality and family status were exact opposites. If that was not enough to initiate a constant family feud, Esau was the favorite of their father and Jacob was the favorite of their mother. Chicanery, opportunity and deceit enabled Jacob to extract the birthright from his older brother. Esau did not take kindly to such treatment from Jacob and later loathed Jacob for what he did. Having tricked his father and "ticked off" his brother, Jacob and his mother decided it was an ideal time for him to visit their distant kin in another country.

Not only were the twins radically different in appearance and personality but also in lifestyle.

Esau acted like a typical Bedouin chief with no property other than his weapon, living off wild game and whatever he plundered from his neighbors. On the other hand, Jacob seemed more civilized and was more like a nomadic shepherd with a tent and a flock. Jacob represented the more developed social order and that was possibly why his mother favored him. Talk about a dysfunctional family! This one wins the prize. They repeatedly broke every conceivable rule in the book for family unity and stability. If we are searching for a family to emulate, this is not the ideal. Why is such a sad saga contained in sacred scripture? Why would anyone carefully preserve the intricate details of a dysfunctional family in the litany of Israel's founding fathers?

Could it be that this is a rather accurate account of a somewhat ordinary family that God used? God did not need special, extraordinary families to accomplish his purpose and promise. As usually, God took the ordinary and affected the extraordinary! God was at work in the common places and people, his wonders to perform. Perhaps the author(s) used the story to emphasize the power of God even in the midst of dysfunctional families and adverse circumstances. Could it be this story is a forceful reminder that God is always larger then any family, regardless of its size, status and sin?

Perhaps the actual existence of such a family is not the issue here. Biblical and secular stories from this period of history reflect a struggle between two lifestyles. There was a great debate, perhaps even violent conflict, over which lifestyle was more appropriate. Some argued that the nomadic life was divinely ordained for Israel. Others were persuaded that she was destined to settle in one place and inhabit the land promised to her. The story of Jacob and Esau may reflect some of that argument and struggle with Isaac and Esau representing one side and Rebekah and Jacob the other.

Could it be that this story is about something else? Historical records from that time chronicle the birth of two nations, Israel and Edom. Those historical records duplicate many of the particulars personified in the above biblical passage and story.

A distinct hint of this possibility appears in the Lord's response to Rebekah's prayer. The Lord told her two nations were in her womb, one would be the stronger, and the older would serve the younger. Some will argue that the Lord foretold the future of Jacob and Esau prior to their birth. Others say the author used the story to relate other significant historical data.

Be that as it may, we are wise to examine closely the corresponding records concerning Edom and Israel. We begin by noting the names given the twins. Each name is a play on words, a practice far more prevalent in ancient times than in our day. "Esau" means red or hairy. It can be connected to "Seir," the place inhabited by the Edomites, located south-east of the Dead Sea where the dirt was red. Tradition indicates that Esau was the leader of the Edomites who lived on Mt. Seir, in the red country. Genesis 32:3 states that Jacob sent greetings to Esau in Seir, the country of Edom. Following their confrontation, Esau began his return trip to Seir (Gen. 33:16). There are undoubtedly numerous chapters in the Jacob-Esau saga of which we have little or no knowledge. Evidence indicates Esau rose to prominence and made his fortune in Sier while Jacob worked to pay for his two wives and made his fortune in another foreign land? Historically speaking, Edom existed long before Israel came into existence. Edom, like Esau, was the first born.

Edom had exercised power and influence. Over time and through unknown circumstances, she lost her dominant position, possibly to Israel or else Israel was blamed for it. At least, Edom's power and influence diminished and Israel's increased. The older nation eventually served the younger, as predicted in the biblical story. Apparently, Edom believed the young and undeserving Israel improperly acquired Edom's "birthright" for power. Therefore, Edom and Israel were at odds, if not war. The life and behavior of Jacob may parallel in some measure the history of Israel. "Jacob" is certainly no saintly name. It can mean "he takes by the heel," "he supplants," "one who over reaches," "one who trips up," and much later in life, "God's protector." The first four descriptive phrases aptly describe the behavior of Jacob in the story and also of Israel in her formative years and beyond.

The characteristics of each country generally resemble the personality of a twin. Edom represented the wild, plundering nation and Israel represented the more advanced and settled social order. The two levels of culture apparently created tremendous and continuous conflict between nations and communities during that period of history. It is highly possible that cultural difference and personal lifestyles fueled the fight between Edom and Israel, just as it seemingly did between Jacob and Esau. National, social and family disarray are duplicated and/or depicted in the story of Jacob and Esau.

Stories reflecting the similarities between two nations and two men may serve more than one purpose. Those kinds of stories depict and preserve an outline easily recalled when retelling important information about a family or nations, if not both at the same time. Family and national history became so intertwined we know not where one ends and the other begins, if and when they do. If nothing else, this saga provides a plausible explanation for the animosity between Edom and Israel, as well as Jacob and Esau. When someone sought an explanation for the continuous hostility, this story provided an acceptable answer. We have modern parallels of important questions receiving acceptable answers that are incorrect. For instance, intelligent children ask, "From where do babies come?" Supposedly intelligent parents reply, "The stork brings them." Could there be some similarity to the reason for the Jacob and Esau saga? Important questions demanded answers and this saga provides some, whether historically correct or not.

Could it be that this story seeks to call special attention to God's power in situations commonly considered hopeless? Apparently, Isaac and Rebekah were considered very old and hopelessly barren but they prayed for an offspring. Who would ever expect such an old couple to have a new baby? Under normal circumstances and with normal people, it is never expected. The author admonishes such disbelief and affirms the power of God, even in common and uncomfortable conditions.

This is another verse of the same biblical song, sung time and time again. God's power frequently exceeds the limits humanity sets. Aging and previously barren women repeatedly found special favor with God and gave birth to a child. Recall the stories about Sara, Rachael, Hanna, Sampson's mother, the mother of John the Baptist, etc. Several significant characters were born to mothers assumed well beyond childbearing age. But not so with Jesus who, according to Matthew and Luke, was born to a young virgin, once more denying the limits set by humanity.

Could it be that the author(s) gave a backhand slap to and a word of hope for Israel? She was growing old and had become religiously barren. She had strayed from the faith and had failed to fulfill her covenant with God. Had she begun to believe there was no hope for her to fulfill her promise to God or God's promise to her? This story vividly reminded Israel of her failure and offered firm assurance that God can give new life to the faithful, regardless of chronological age. Regardless of her failures or present condition, Israel could be an instrument of God. She need not remain barren.

Could it be there is at least one more purpose for this story, whether originally intended or not? In addition to the above possible purposes, or maybe because of them, this is also our story. Change the names, date and particular circumstances and we are right in the midst of it. It is as modern as the morning news or our last family feud. The possible ramifications and individual applications of this ancient and modern story are too numerous and personal to mention all of them. We have been or have had a bothersome brother (sister). Many of us fought over "who gets what" during childhood years and the settlement of the family estate. Having seen something we really wanted, we sought it by whatever means necessary.

More than once we traded something of great value for almost worthless junk. Most often it was far more important than marbles, tea sets and Aunt Jane's biscuit bowl. We encountered something we wanted more than what we had. Much of what we had was ours by birth but we saw no real value in it at the time.

Having traded it or simply given it away, it could never be ours again as it had originally been. Even if it was partially restored, it was somewhat tainted. So were we. To one degree or another, our good name, sexual purity, hard earned dollars, valuable time, gentle words, helping hands, contented conscious, etc. were often traded away for a moment of pleasure or in a futile attempt to pacify our appetite for lesser things.

Could it be that this story waves a warning flag in the face of our first love, what we love more than anything else? The entire family in this biblical story seems to suffer from misplaced values and improper love. Their pursuit of them was the seedbed for serious difficulties. The parents' favoritism for one child fostered family hostility. Jacob's compelling desire for his father's special blessing and extra inheritance caused him to do dastardly deeds. Esau's craving for nothing more than good food was so important at that moment he lost track of his family status and responsibility. Rebekah's smothering love for Jacob encouraged his and her deceit. It is always like that. Whatever we love most always gets our best effort and major energy, even when we deny its importance. Such truth is too significant to remain hidden in a story we first thought irrelevant.

Could it be this is our story in another sense? It speaks to us about the possible removal of our barren behavior in the faith, about the restoration of our covenant with God. That should be our first love! In our dysfunctional, thoughtless and sinful condition, we cannot restore our birthright or produce new life, but God can. What once appeared foul and fallow ground can be restored to productivity when God works in us. The average and ordinary become the special and spectacular when God comes to us and uses us for his purposes. Make no mistake! This is our story too, from the beginning to the end.

The story of Jacob and Esau is a wonderful story of great significance, especially when we see it from a new perspective. It shines a spotlight on us and enables us to see ourselves for what we are. We often imitate both brothers whose selfishness gets us into serious difficulties. We are called to be like them in forgiveness of those who misused or abused us. It tells us God uses imperfect people for his purposes. It proclaims personal hope for us, regardless of what we have been. Having seen all that, we are more likely to see that ordinary people like us are also God's children who have hope and promise.

CHAPTER THREE
A Catalogue of Questions
Genesis 3: 1-19

1: Now the serpent was more subtle than any other wild creature that the LORD God had made. He said to the woman, "Did God say, "You shall not eat of any tree of the garden'?"

2: And the woman said to the serpent, "We may eat of the fruit of the trees of the garden;

3: but God said," You shall not eat of the fruit of the tree which is in the midst of the garden, neither shall you touch it, lest you die."

4: But the serpent said to the woman, "You will not die.

5: For God knows that when you eat of it your eyes will be opened, and you will be like God, knowing good and evil."

6: So when the woman saw that the tree was good for food, and that it was a delight to the eyes, and that the tree was to be desired to make one wise, she took of its fruit and ate; and she also gave some to her husband, and he ate.

7: Then the eyes of both were opened, and they knew that they were naked; and they sewed fig leaves together and made themselves aprons.

8: And they heard the sound of the LORD God walking in the garden in the cool of the day, and the man and his wife hid themselves from the presence of the LORD God among the trees of the garden.

9: But the LORD God called to the man, and said to him, "Where are you?"

10: And he said, "I heard the sound of thee in the garden, and I was afraid, because I was naked; and I hid myself."

11: He said, "Who told you that you were naked? Have you eaten of the tree of which I commanded you not to eat?"

12: The man said, "The woman whom thou gavest to be with me, she gave me fruit of the tree, and I ate."

13: Then the LORD God said to the woman, "What is this that you have done?" The woman said, "The serpent beguiled me, and I ate."

14: The LORD God said to the serpent, "Because you have done this, cursed are you above all cattle, and above all wild animals; upon your belly you shall go, and dust you shall eat all the days of your life.

15: I will put enmity between you and the woman, and between your seed and her seed; he shall bruise your head, and you shall bruise his heel."

16: To the woman he said, "I will greatly multiply your pain in childbearing; in pain you shall bring forth children, yet your desire shall be for your husband, and he shall rule over you."

17: And to Adam he said, "Because you have listened to the voice of your wife, and have eaten of the tree of which I commanded you, "You shall not eat of it,' cursed is the ground because of you; in toil you shall eat of it all the days of your life;

18: thorns and thistles it shall bring forth to you; and you shall eat the plants of the field.

19: In the sweat of your face you shall eat bread till you return to the ground, for out of it you were taken; you are dust, and to dust you shall return."

This story is commonly called "The First Temptation" or "The Fall of Man" and deserves careful consideration. It recounts another significant saga remembered and revered by many religious people. For some, it is the bedrock of their beliefs and the final answer to questions in the faith.

From this passage came the fundamental building blocks for much of Apostle Paul's writings recorded in the New Testament. His apparent acceptance of a literal interpretation lies underneath some of his theology. Many of us were taught to accept these stories exactly as written, without further examination or contemplation of what the author was trying to convey.

I shall never say this passage did not happen exactly as recorded. However, I do confess to having difficulty accepting it as a precise and perfect report of historical events. It is another story that presents items and events for which we have no personal point of reference. It leaves us hanging in the air, wondering what its author intended. It tells about a walking and talking snake, weird creatures having body parts resembling both human and beast, plus a God who walks, talks and acts as if he were human. In one way or another, these key elements are the underpinning for the story but provide no reference point from which to interpret it in light of our experiences. That may not always be necessary but its absence often causes us to disregard the story and relegate it to religious fanaticism.

Such a response to this story need not occur. In order to find a more favorable response to it, we need not change the story, only our interpretation of and approach to it. It has some extremely crucial things to say to us but they may be far different than we were taught or had ever thought. This story is about some basic issues seldom seen or discussed by those who cherish it most. In fact, some may cherish it for reasons they never suspected, reasons that may first seem helpful but may eventually prove to be religiously unhealthy.

Could it be that one purpose for this passage was to answer a catalogue of common questions? Like us, ancient religious people wanted answers to fundamental questions about life. Lurking in the background, never openly exposed but obviously there, is a long list of questions which this passage attempts to answer in some form or fashion. Answers are offered for the following obvious questions.

What is the origin of evil? Why do we disobey God? Why does the snake crawl on his belly? Why do we hate snakes? Why do snakes normally inflict their bite on the lower part of our body? Why do we wear clothes? Why do we try to hide from God? Why does humanity have to work for a living? Why is childbirth painful? Why do we die? Could it be that this passage was purposely and specifically designed to answer those questions? Was it a catechism of sorts, used to instruct converts to the faith, both children and adults? Were these questions asked those who professed faith in God and were those persons required to answer correctly? This set of selected and possibly prescribed answers would provide the religious community consistent and reliable answers for themselves and for any non- believer who asked one of those questions.

Such questions cry out for honest answers, but are these answers adequate? Could it be that many deeply religious people, ancient and modern, love this story because is offers simple answers to complicated questions? It comes to the rescue and often fully satisfies religious people who feel they must provide some answer, any
answer, rather than no answer or saying, "I don't know." From their perspective, giving no answer or saying "I don't know" renounces the faith and they refuse to do that. The determination to give some answer may not be as positive as it first seems. Specific answers to all these questions may insinuate we know as much as God by having an exact answer for everything.

Perhaps it is both beneficial and frightening to be reminded that any human answers to these questions are inadequate and incomplete. Answers to these questions are hidden in the mysteries of God and therefore impossible for us to fully understand. The best any of us can do is guess, knowing that our answers are and always will be incomplete and insufficient. If we forget that, we pretend to possess knowledge that is not ours and we make ourselves suspect to those
who know we don't know everything. Whatever answers we give in our guesses should always respect and preserve the inexplicable power and purposefulness of God.

Let us boldly contemplate these difficult questions but quickly confess that our answers are always less than perfect. If eventually we are compelled to admit, "I don't know," it is not because we have no faith but because we have great faith in and a deep awareness of God's indescribable nature. It may be wise and very religious to end by admitting we don't know. Could it be that is where the author of this story began and ended? Could it be that in order to plumb the depths of this passage, we too must humbly say, "I don't know the absolute answer to all these questions?" If we never reach this point, we fail to hear the fundamental messages contained therein. Like the questions lurking in the shadows, its penetrating truths are not overly obvious at the initial reading. We will never fully understand it. By looking carefully, thinking deeply and pondering prayerfully, we will find in it eternal truths applicable to all. Therefore, this story is for us, about us and relevant to us.

Could it be that those who first formulated these words did not take them literally? They undoubtedly knew adequate answers to these questions were hidden in the mysteries of God. They had no intention of giving final answers to unanswerable questions. They sought a symbolic way to say the answers are far beyond us. Like other religions of their day, they chose stories that conveyed what was not literally said in the text. The written words served as an easy way to remember a story that held hidden meaning. The first casual reading was never enough to identify the deep religious truths lurking in the shadows, waiting to be found. It took dedicated effort and deep religious faith to find some of the religious truths proclaimed in the words. Hidden within the shadows of this story is a bold affirmation that God is and always was in control. He consistently acts in his own way and we do not have to understand or approve it.

Could it be that this passage presents the process through which everyone goes when they are truly tempted? It illustrates how temptation's net slowly tightens around us, making escape progressively difficult. Having confronted the temptation, we may first recall what we were originally taught. We hope to find permission to do it or at least no prohibition against doing whatever it is that tempts us.

21

We check to ascertain if what we now remember is what was really said. That step comes early in the passage when the serpent asks the woman to clarify what God really said. You can almost see the synapses of her brain rushing to refresh her memory of earlier admonitions. So it is with us, at least the first few times it comes, whatever the temptation may be. We go through all sorts of gyrations in an effort to negate the prohibition, whether issued by a parent, officer of the law or God. The first step reconfirms the rule. The second step questions the rule itself and may even deny its validity. If someone did say it as we remember, did they have the authority to say it and did they really mean it? This maneuver occurs in our passage when the serpent tells the woman the rule is invalid.

The third step is to conclude the rule is no longer applicable and that we are above the law. The woman is convinced she may eat the fruit and not die, regardless of what the rule and Ruler said. She questions the knowledge and authority of God. There are more ancient and modern illustrations of this step than we know or have time to tell. Each of us had our own personal experience. It is experienced in our disobedience toward our parents, disregard for religious rules and teachings, disobedience of civil laws, business fraud, lies, premarital sex, marital infidelity, failure to love God above all else and then our neighbors as our self, etc. It is always the same. We confirm the law's existence, question its authority and conclude iti s not applicable for us. The fourth indicator that temptation's net has almost completely caught us is a strong desire for what we do not have. A burning desire may provide strong support for denying the law's validity. That attitude is easily identified in our passage. The woman wanted to be like God, with infinite knowledge and all the privileges pertaining there to. The primary principle is the same for us. We selfishly want something and we want it now! We can even justify having it. "So what if God, Mom, the church, the state or anyone else says I should not have it. Times have drastically changed, so what do they know? They just want its pleasures for themselves or don't want me to have any fun. I am entitled to it just as they are. I want to be just like them." Having reached this juncture, it is difficult to resist the temptation and the net tightens around us.

captures us in the fifth and final step. We assure ourselves that the end result will be most delightful, fully satisfying and without any painful repercussions. Our passage speaks of the woman's delight in recognizing the forbidden fruit was good for food, beautiful to behold, and would make her wonderfully wise. She not only tasted it but also "cooked a pot of it to feed her husband." Her story is often our story because we imitate her actions.

She was partially correct in her judgment. Forbidden fruit frequently has a temporary pleasant taste, may be beautiful to behold and teaches us something we did not previously know. Partaking of forbidden fruit opens our eyes to the experience of disobedience, deceit, shame, guilt, etc. Disobedience, and all forbidden fruit, frequently teaches us something but what it teaches is never of equal value to what we could have learned had we remained obedient. It also teaches us by providing something it never promised. It carries a hidden virus in its pocket that soon punctures our genuine pleasure, blemishes our internal beauty and bashes us against basic truth. Partaking of forbidden fruit definitely opens our eyes but at a tremendous cost.

Could it be that this passage seeks to show us humanity's common response following exposure of failure? Learning that their disobedience produced unpleasant consequences, the man and woman tried to hide. Their disobedience destroyed their relationship with God and each other. It created an additional gulf between them. Disobedience has an inescapable consequence because it always establishes a gulf that previously was not there. The existence of that gulf and the accompanying presence of guilt and pain are demonstrated by unwise thoughts and behavior. The man and woman made matters worse by foolishly making clothes out of fig leaves. Friends, if you know anything about ordinary fig leaves, you know the foolishness of covering your private parts with prickly and scratchy leaves whose milky sap can irritate like poison ivy. Foolishness personified, and we are no different! Our deliberate disobedience and flimsy excuses make about as much sense as the clothing made from fig leaves or an attempt to hide from God. Each is uncomfortable, foolish and of little lasting value.

Our passage repeatedly illustrates human response when our disobedience is discovered. We place the blame for our failure on another or something else and assume no personal responsibility. The man blamed the woman and she blamed the snake. Look closely in the passage and you will notice the man also blamed God because every item, including snake, fruit, woman and man, is God's creation. In essence, the man said, "Don't blame me. You created me and I have to deal with what you gave me." Note the subtlety of the author's suggestion that the origin of evil is actually hidden in the mysteries of God because he made everything. Not written but possibly implied in the passage, God expected the man and woman to use the powers they possessed to obey the rules designed fort heir good. They were held accountable for their decisions and behavior because God gave them ability to choose. That message and this passage are about us because we continue to blame others for our misdeeds. Others may lead us into temptation but we are primarily responsible for our response.

Could it be that this passage emphasizes our temptation to focus primarily on "self"? It also illustrates the folly of such behavior. The characters in the cast keep asking "What's in it for me?" or "How can I get what I want?" Nothing and no one else seemed important to them. Rules made by others were in their way and they considered their selfish desires more important to them than obedience to "useless" rules. The man and woman decided to make new rules so there would be no disobedience. Thinking highly of themselves, they decided they knew more than God and would no longer rely on his wisdom and rules. In short, they sought to usurp God's place. Were they not as we are? We are one with them in having been tempted to be the center of our world and then we are separated from each other by yielding to it. The temptation to value "self" above all else slides into our midst with the subtlety of a slippery snake. It promises a delightful abundance of knowledge, power, and pleasure. Its half truths entice us. Our passage tells us the greatest temptation of all is to "be God," which is the highest form of idolatry. Humanity's attempts to "play God" have produced more hellish results than any other thing. Read the passage again and see us. However, we need a reminder that a high and healthy opinion of self is crucial for a wholesome and productive life.

The difficult trick is to find a proper balance between too much and not enough self-esteem.

Our passage repeatedly points to the folly, or stupidity, of usurping power that is not rightfully ours. It reminds us that self-will and rebellion eventually confront the sovereign will and power of God. There is and always will be something bigger than self-will. Sooner or later, we must deal with it or get destroyed by it. Those who believe otherwise will eventually either change their mind or get crushed by those eternal laws for life. The man, woman and serpent each attempted to take God's place but he remained in control. This biblical story repeatedly states, "Don't mess with God. If you do, you will lose." The passage cautions us to be ever alert for sneaky "snakes" (subtle and enticing temptations) that entice us to "play God" and we must be ready to "bash their heads" when discovered in our midst. Otherwise, they lead us astray.

Could it be that this passage offers other eternal truths that at least deserve honorable mention? First, when God asks where we are, it is not because he is uninformed. He calls not to locate us but so we may properly locate ourselves in relation to him. Having deliberately chosen to separate ourselves from him and each other, he reminds us that he is still in the neighborhood. His grace enables a renewed relationship with him and one another but it must be on his terms. Our disobedience does not destroy him, his rules or his willingness to give us another chance. It only destroys us!

Secondly, the serpent was teetering on the edge of truth. We can be somewhat like God if we choose. Being able to do so comes not from self-pronouncement or mutiny but from the created order God instituted. In order to become more like God we must submit to his will, not usurp it or dethrone him. In submitting, we are given some knowledge of good and evil, but never ultimate knowledge, which by necessity must be reserved only for God. Joyful submission will open our eyes and we will be able to discern some degree of good and evil. In submitting to God's will, we act, in a small way, like God.

Our being and action vaguely imitate his being and action. He created us to be somewhat like him, not to replace him. Thirdly, our passage tells us there are several kinds and degrees of death. It is not limited to the cessation of breathing. Breaking life- giving rules inflicts death of some kind and in some manner. There is death of innocence, trust, inner peace, relationships, honesty, integrity, etc. This kind of death may sometimes provide knowledge not previously known but the process of acquiring it is extremely painful and dangerous. Knowing can be more painful than not knowing! Having learned through experience, we know disobedience hurts and destroys. Thanks be to God, this kind of death and destruction is not necessarily final nor is it as powerful as God. In spite of our slap in his face, God continually visits our jungle, calls to let us know where we are and to help us repair the damage. He offers to clothe us with grace and forgiveness instead of the scratchyf ig leaves we may deserve.

Could it be that this story is one of the greatest passages of the Bible? It is precisely that, not because it gives simple and understandable answers to unanswerable questions but because it deals with major issues we daily confront. It does answer fundamental questions but not those we first thought. Simple answers, strange creatures, and a slippery snake are basically unimportant to its real message. If we get overly concerned about and enamored with the former, we will almost certainly miss a major portion of the message. If we have previously regarded this passage as irrelevant and irreligious, it is time to examine it from this new perspective.

CHAPTER FOUR
Muddy Waters
Exodus 14: 5-31

5: When the king of Egypt was told that the people had fled, the mind of Pharaoh and his servants was changed toward the people, and they said, "What is this we have done, that we have let Israel go from serving us?"

6: So he made ready his chariot and took his army with him,

7: and took six hundred picked chariots and all the other chariots of Egypt with officers over all of them.

8: And the LORD hardened the heart of Pharaoh king of Egypt and he pursued the people of Israel as they went forth defiantly.

9: The Egyptians pursued them, all Pharaoh's horses and chariots and his horsemen and his army, and overtook them encamped at the sea, by Pi-ha-hi'roth, in front of Ba'al-ze'phon.

10: When Pharaoh drew near, the people of Israel lifted up their eyes, and behold, the Egyptians were marching after them; and they were in great fear. And the people of Israel cried out to the LORD;

11: and they said to Moses, "Is it because there are no graves in Egypt that you have taken us away to die in the wilderness? What have you done to us, in bringing us out of Egypt?

12: Is not this what we said to you in Egypt,"Let us alone and let us serve the Egyptians'? For it would have been better for us to serve the Egyptians than to die in the wilderness."

13: And Moses said to the people, "Fear not, stand firm, and see the salvation of the LORD, which he will work for you today; for the Egyptians whom you see today, you shall never see again.

14: The LORD will fight for you, and you have only to be still."

15: The LORD said to Moses, "Why do you cry to me? Tell the people of Israel to go forward.

16: Lift up your rod, and stretch out your hand over the sea and divide it, that the people of Israel may go on dry ground through the sea.

17: And I will harden the hearts of the Egyptians so that they shall go in after them, and I will get glory over Pharaoh and all his host, his chariots, and his horsemen.

18: And the Egyptians shall know that I am the LORD, when I have gotten glory over Pharaoh, his chariots, and his horsemen."

19: Then the angel of God who went before the host of Israel moved and went behind them; and the pillar of cloud moved from before them and stood behind them,

20: coming between the host of Egypt and the host of Israel. And there was the cloud and the darkness; and the night passed without one coming near the other all night.

21: Then Moses stretched out his hand over the sea; and the LORD drove the sea back by a strong east wind all night, and made the sea dry land, and the waters were divided.

22: And the people of Israel went into the midst of the sea on dry ground, the waters being a wall to them on their right hand and on their left.

23: The Egyptians pursued, and went in after them into the midst of the sea, all Pharaoh's horses, his chariots, and his horsemen.

24: And in the morning watch the LORD in the pillar of fire and of cloud looked down upon the host of the Egyptians, and discomfited the host of the Egyptians,

25: clogging their chariot wheels so that they drove heavily; and the Egyptians said, "Let us flee from before Israel; for the LORD fights for them against the Egyptians."

26: Then the LORD said to Moses, "Stretch out your hand over the sea, that the water may come back upon the Egyptians, upon their chariots, and upon their horsemen."

27: So Moses stretched forth his hand over the sea, and the sea returned to its wonted flow when the morning appeared; and the Egyptians fled into it, and the LORD routed the Egyptians in the midst of the sea.

28: The waters returned and covered the chariots and the horsemen and all the host of Pharaoh that had followed them into the sea; not so much as one of them remained.

29: But the people of Israel walked on dry ground through the sea, the waters being a wall to them on their right hand and on their left.

30: Thus the LORD saved Israel that day from the hand of the Egyptians; and Israel saw the Egyptians dead upon the seashore.

31: And Israel saw the great work which the LORD did against the Egyptians, and the people feared the LORD; and they believed in the LORD and in his servant Moses.

The biblical story commonly called "The Crossing of the Red Sea" is one whose particulars cannot be verified but whose momentous impact must not be denied. It is another biblical saga that, on a first or casual reading, seems to have little connection to the world in which we live. A close and careful examination, along with additional information, will quickly reveal the errors of that first assumption. Some of our present confusion comes from our inability to identify the exact spot or even the general area where this event took place. The geographic identifiers in the story do not identify any known locations. Other historical records of that era provide no help. Our information is as clear as muddy water! We have another serious problem. How do we properly interpret the word "sea?" Its biblical usage means different things at different times. It can mean a body of salt water, a fresh water lake, a river, or even a moist depression. Using that as a definition, there were numerous "seas" in Egypt. A search for the "Red Sea," sometimes identified as the "Sea of Reeds," provides no specific location. Some scholars believe "Red Sea" should be translated "Papyrus Lake." Since papyrus apparently grew only in fresh water, this would indicate an inland location.

Wherever it was, what was Moses doing there? From what we are able to determine from the story, the Israelites were fleeing from the Egyptians. Suddenly, they ceased running and apparently camped in a spot similar to a box canyon. We are led to believe, like many participants in the story, they had little or no hope for escape. It seems as if the people fully expected to be killed or to become Egyptian slaves once more.

Our answer to why they were there and in that predicament hinges on other presuppositions that can be neither denied nor proven. Some of those who were trapped thought it was due to the stupidity of Moses and their unwise dependence on him. There are those who argue that Moses deliberately set a trap for Pharaoh's army but did not inform the other Israelites. Some deeply religious folk among us think God put them in that tough spot so they would fully trust him after he demonstrated protective power. Other open-minded people say it illustrates how our deliberate choices can easily back us into a corner, regardless of how hard we try to avoid it. Still others say this is a common experience for everyone because we all eventually find ourselves in a position that demands outside help in order to receive deliverance from the encroaching enemy.

Could it be the author had little concern with telling exactly why or how the Israelites got where they were? His primary interest was telling how Israel ultimately became a powerful nation with a powerful religion. The miraculous deliverance was fully attributed to the power of God and that spectacular deliverance made an indeliblei mprint on their minds and religious faith. Their escape from their enemy was the identifying moment in the life and history of Israel. The Israelites eventually came to view deliverance as the most significant event of their history, an event and an experience that they would remember and recite. This event is to the Old Testament what Christ is to the New Testament. Each gives meaning to what came before and after. Without a spectacular deliverance, there would be no need to remember Israel's history nor would the rest ofi t make sense. Everything prior to this escape brought them to that place. Everything that followed always depends on and points back to what God did for them at that time and location. It can only be identified as a revelatory and redeeming act of God that no mortal can fully describe or define. So, it is with Christ! The story of her deliverance may be Israel's song of praise and thanksgiving to God who brought her from the muddy waters of slavery and death and established her on dry land.

Could it be that this story is a personification of a historical epic that enables quick recall and recitation of an event(s) that must never be forgotten? Since biblical writers often employed that method to convey and emphasize a basic truth, this story could be another example. This possibility has some merit because we have almost no specific answers to where, when, or why. A careful reading of the story indicates that it could have been embellished through repeated telling. If this story exemplifies that practice and purpose, our inquiry into "how" and "why" raises specific questions and looks for definitive answers never intended by this story. Could it be this story is a historical summary or a small portion of an actual and longer event in Israel's history? Could it tell how some natural phenomenon was extremely helpful in delivering the Israelites from their enemy? This story provides strong hints that thunder, lightning, fire and smoke were present. Could it have rained on the Egyptians but not on the Israelites? Was there a severe thunderstorm that frightened, confused and devastated the enemy as the torrential rain filled moist depressions with deep and muddy water, making them impassable for Pharaoh's chariots? Narrow rims on heavy chariots carrying two or three strong men soon sank into soft soil, especially if one chariot followed in the tracks of another. If this event occurred during dry weather, were the reeds along the shore set on fire by the Israelites, or maybe by lightening? Did thick smoke blind, choke and confuse the Egyptians while the fire gave light to the Israelites for travel during darkness? Did the Israelites hide during the day behind or in the smoke? Did the smoke and fire provide protection and more time to properly prepare for their intended crossing?

Could it be there were several different escapes and different conditions primarily responsible for each success? One escape may have resulted from the use of smoke and fire while another took advantage of a thunder storm, etc. Were there unsuccessful escape attempts? Perhaps stories about the different successful escape experiences were eventually woven into one. The story was not told to identify the exact process through which they went but to boldly affirm that God made escape possible. That was the most important part of the story and the reason for relating it. For them and us, it is much more remarkable if God used ordinary items to accomplish spectacular results. If God accomplished a spectacular deliverance by using ordinary things, he will most likely do it again!

Could it be the "darkness" mentioned in the story may mean more than the absence of natural light? Was the darkness in the minds of the Egyptians who did not know the ways of God? Is it possible that Egyptian warriors were not bright and consequently easily trapped or deceived? Did they have no eagerness to pursue the enemy? Conversely, were the Israelites suffering from mental slowness or were they enlightened about the will of God and eager to escape? Were they enlightened about effective warfare and did they know how to take advantage of marshlands and smoking reeds?

We can believe a natural process provided the catalyst for deliverance without changing any part of the story and without denying the miraculous activities of God. If we can accept the possibility that the catalyst was a natural phenomenon, we remove the event from the category of a "once in a lifetime occurrence for someone special" and place it in the midst of our every day world. Having done that, we once more affirm that the God of ancient Israel can and does come to our aid in the common things of life.

I do not know all the particulars behind this story. The natural phenomenon theory does not disturb me, as long as the activity of God remains the primary focal point. Even if the water receded through some unusual but natural phenomenon, it was still an act of God. I witnessed an event in which something similar may have occurred. I served as pastor of Leggett Memorial United Methodist Church in Biloxi, MS. Directly out my office window and across a major thoroughfare was the Gulf of Mexico. Day after day I observed the water lapping at the sea wall just beyond the roadway. Without advanced warning, the strangest thing happened. The water mysteriously receded several hundred yards from the sea wall. The water and wet sand were no longer at their normal location. I could have safely driven my "motorized chariot" hundreds of feet from the regular shoreline. The situation soon changed. Within a few hours, the wheels of my chariot would have become inundated by the muddy water or mired in the mud and wet sand at their usual location.

I was told a fierce wind, strange tidal activities and other natural causes resulted in that unusual occurrence. If strong Mississippi winds can drive back the water in the Gulf, then the Sirocco winds can do the same thing to a body of water in Egypt. If that Mississippi experience of unexpected dry land had liberated someone from impending danger or death, it would no doubt have made a lasting and dramatic impression on them.

They too would look back, marvel at the miracle from God and proudly tell others their story of salvation and deliverance. I also witnessed a somewhat similar phenomenon in another climate and under very different conditions. As an Air Force Chaplain, I regularly visited troops along the Bering Straits in northern Alaska. The Arctic ice was mysterious, powerful and unpredictable. Subzero temperature produced ice several feet thick. It was strong enough to easily support an airplane on which I was a passenger and a large bulldozer that took a shortcut into town. The changing tides, strong wind and other natural cause often separated huge chunks of ice, called ice flows, from the shore and later returned them, but never to their original position. Chunks of ice, from small pieces up to several miles long and wide, frequently floated in the unfrozen water beneath. Some scholars surmise that early inhabitants got to America, either by riding a huge ice flow or by walking across while the ice was attached to the shore. If someone was miraculous delivered from danger or death by crossing the Bering Sea on a "dry" ice flow, could that be considered somewhat similar to crossing the Red Sea on dry ground? Could it be this passage speaks of sincere faith and universal behavior that demands recognition and response by anyone who seeks to serve God? It admonishes us to remain steadfast when we are on an errand for God? In spite of all the mumbling and grumbling from his followers, Moses never wavered in his faith or the determination to continue the task before him. This does not address the matter of identifying a true mission for God. It does suggest we must never judge the worth of a mission by its use of ordinary things or abandon it simply because it is fraught with personal danger. The above point is illustrated by my support of the Civil Rights Movement in Mississippi during the 1960's. Without absolute proof, a group of us were convinced we were on the side of ultimate truth and on a mission for God. We could have quietly embraced the cause without publicly declaring support, like numerous other clergy in the area.

Like Moses, we felt we could not be faithful in our service to God by taking the easy way out. We were in a "box canyon" but we did not turn back, even when our congregations complained vehemently, publicly branded us infidels, threatened to withhold our salary and possibly kill us. The Israelites held no monopoly on slavery, harsh criticism, contempt and danger. Mudslinging was the chief weapon of our opponents and they desperately sought to mire us in it. Lies were printed in the newspapers about us. We were harassed and hated, repeatedly threatened, run off from our churches, and eventually denied pastoral appointments even though the law of the church said we must be assigned.

Having gone through that ordeal, I believe I have first hand knowledge of what Moses experienced. The opposition sought to entrap and enslave me in the sea of hate and harassment. The storm clouds of death threats and family danger constantly hovered. I cannot describe or explain it but I was never terribly afraid. Like Moses, I did not know how deliverance would come, or if it would come, but an unwavering faith in God kept me from turning back. I believed I was doing God's will and that he would either protect me or use my death to further his cause.

The catalyst for my deliverance was a natural phenomenon but I call it a miracle from God. The Air Force had an unexpected vacancy for a Methodist chaplain. Unusual events and circumstances facilitated my application and selection for that position. For years, I had wanted to be an Air Force Chaplain. I could be a chaplain, maintain my affiliation with the church in Mississippi and continue to witness for integration.

The basic point of my personal deliverance is strikingly similar to Israel's. Could it be that every story of true deliverance is patterned after Israel's because that is the way God works? He most often shuns cataclysmic events and one-of-a-kind miracles in favor of using ordinary items and events to accomplish great things. Perhaps God repeatedly delivered us from serious danger by some natural event and we did not know it. Israel's story is our story too. Could it be that this story provides resplendent examples of human tendencies, if not human nature? Chief among them is blaming others for our present location or status, even though we asked, or possibly begged, them to help us get where we are. We may have even voted for the procedure they followed but when failure seemed apparent, we could only criticize, condemn and blame others. We lose faith in the leader and give up on the cause. The Israelites were not the last people to play the "Let you and him fight" game. For them, Moses was "IT" and the outcome was up to him. Others assumed no responsibility for the fight, offered no encouragement and provided no support. That sounds very modern! Another human tendency is to lose hope and surrender to the opposition in the face of impending danger, like many of the Israelites in this story. Judeo-Christian living does not allow such behavior. Biblical heroes, Christian martyrs and noted secular leaders never did that. Their willingness to die for the cause was the impetus for success and if they died, their death was the rallying cry for those who followed. Moses and Jesus are excellent examples for us.

When it became apparent that each Israelite might have to fend for himself/herself, they thought slavery was better than death in the wilderness. During various periods and events in human history, others were of the same opinion, expressed either in word or actions. Many in America thought it was better to be a slave to existing social conditions than to bear the necessary pain in the fight for freedom, desegregation, etc. Who spoke against the humiliation and slaughter of the Native Americans, Hitler's killing of the Jews and the South's treatment of African Americans? Who led the fight against sexual abuse in churches, homes and streets? In every case, it was often considered easier to remain a slave to the system than to fight for everyone's freedom. The few who spoke against such practices often led an unpredictable life and some met a painful death, but they lived and died in real freedom. Similar battles are now in progress or are yet to be fought. Some prefer slavery rather than pay the price of freedom…in this biblical story and in our day.

Could this story be a vivid reminder that humanity's power and mental capacity are, never have been and never will be superior to God's? God has blessed us with an abundance of both. When we depend only on them, we inevitably find ourselves in a box canyon with no human means of escape. It is only God's gracious acts that can set us free. We may or may not be aware of divine deliverance. We sometimes call it a natural phenomenon, good luck, personal ability or attribute it to another person. Each or all of these may have had a part in our deliverance but those of deep faith know that God works in mysterious ways. God's assisting angels did not close shop once the Israelites escaped Egypt. God's special angels often take human form. They prayerfully provide seen and unseen assistance, lead simple or saintly lives and point us to the real source of ultimate power.

Could this passage be a reminder of something we already know but do not want to admit? Regardless of our situation or condition, we have some responsibility for effecting a change. Moses declared that fact when he said, "Go forward." He had carried them as far as he could. Deliverance could come only if they moved forward. They had probably spent much time in prayer and meditation but the time for action was at hand. There is a time to pray and a time to act. Without the latter, the former may be shallow or selfish. In genuine prayer, the latter may be more of the former than we first thought. Iti s always surprising to discover what we can do when we want to do it and are assured it is the right thing to do. A portion of all success, both the Israelites' and ours, always depends on the readiness and willingness to act when the time is right. God does not wait on us forever!

Could it be this passage offers a valuable lesson about mud? I have lived in an area with an abundance of disgusting "gumbo" mud. It firmly sticks to anything that comes in contact with it: shoes, garden tools, lawn mower wheels, etc. It doesn't just stick. Through repeated contacts, it keeps sticking and collecting until it debilitates everything to which it easily attaches. If Egypt's mud was anything like this mud, I understand why Pharaoh's chariots were useless. Moses may have perfectly understood the characteristics of sticky mud. The fact that the Israelites "crossed on dry ground" has much greater significance if you know anything about gumbo mud. Perhaps part of the miracle is that Moses, a country boy, knew where and when the land was dry but the Egyptians, the city slickers, didn't. Perhaps the references to mud in this passage are both literal and symbolic. It suggests certain characteristics of evil whose properties are very similar to gumbo mud. Evil pursuit always causes problems. Those who continually participate in it progressively have more and more of it attached to them. Evil, like gumbo mud, sticks and clings until it becomes debilitating, to one degree or another. It eventually clogs the wheels of falsehood's chariots and ultimately brings to a halt those who seek to live a lie.

God does not necessarily destroy those who continually "play in the mud." They choose to destroy themselves! According to the laws of creation, destruction is the inevitable result for all who choose to deny God's supremacy. It seems their mud often sticks to others. For numerous reasons, we may accidentally or deliberately choose to walk in the mud. Sometimes, we are forced to walk there. Regardless of where or how we collected our personal mud, it may become necessary for us to wade in the water to wash it away and then travel on dry land. Water isn't always bad! However, the opportunity to walk and remain on dry land is an apt description of deliverance from all that would inflict evil upon us.

Anyone who doubts the relevancy of this passage should carefully read it again. It is an intriguing story about deliverance for the Israelites and it foreshadows our own deliverance from so much that would harm us. Deliverance is always the gift of God and it makes little difference if the conduit is called ordinary or indescribable. The Israelites recognized the impact of this divine deliverance and considered it the high point of their history. If we have experienced divine deliverance, that is also a high point in our history which we frequently recall and joyfully retell. This story is also about us and for us.

CHAPTER FIVE
JITTERS AT THE JABBOK
Genesis 32:22-30

22: The same night he arose and took his two wives, his two maids, and his eleven children, and crossed the ford of the Jabbok.

23: He took them and sent them across the stream, and likewise everything that he had.

24: And Jacob was left alone; and a man wrestled with him until the breaking of the day.

25: When the man saw that he did not prevail against Jacob, he touched the hollow of his thigh; and Jacob's thigh was put out of joint as he wrestled with him.

26: Then he said, "Let me go, for the day is breaking." But Jacob said, "I will not let you go, unless you bless me."

27: And he said to him, "What is your name?" And he said, "Jacob."

28: Then he said, "Your name shall no more be called Jacob, but Israel, for you have striven with God and with men, and have prevailed."

29: Then Jacob asked him, "Tell me, I pray, your name." But he said, "Why is it that you ask my name?" And there he blessed him.

30: So Jacob called the name of the place Peni'el, saying, "For I have seen God face to face, and yet my life is preserved."
Jacob had a severe case of the jitters the night he camped by the Jabbok River. He was on the run again, this time from a furious father-in-law. To make matters even worse, he received news that Esau, his estranged brother, was in front of him and prepared to "greet" him on the other side of the river. Jacob was trapped between the two people who had reasons to hate him most. He was in a precarious situation because he knew not what to expect from either direction.

Apparently, the two brothers had not seen each other since Jacob, many years earlier, surreptitiously seized the family birthright and suddenly departed on an extended vacation to a foreign land. That vacation had recently and abruptly ended, due to Jacob's questionable activity with his father-in-law's flock.

Jacob did not have the upper hand this time. His mother was not running interference or calling the next play from the sideline. Esau had not declared his intentions. Jacob's and Laban's known deceit gave no guidance, justification or suggestion for Jacob's next move. Jacob was alone and afraid. In spite of the fact that Jacob had earlier appropriated Esau's portion of the family fortune, both brothers had prospered. Each had a sizable family, herd and fortune with them. We have no explanation of how Esau accumulated his wealth but we do have strong hints that Jacob prospered from "ill-gotten gain." Caught between the two from whom he had taken much, Jacob probably pondered the wild oats he had sewn in the family soil and wondered if one of his kin, or both, would initiate the harvest. Anxious, agitated, and alone in a strange place, Jacob lay down by the river to sleep. Our passage clearly indicates he rested very little because he was involved in a horrendous wrestling match during much of the long night. It does not clearly state with whom he wrestled. Jacob's opponent is first identified as a man, then as a spirit who could not endure the dawn and eventually as God. We are left wondering if it was only one of these or all three. Without more information, we must imagine what transpired, and with whom, the night Jacob had the jitters by the Jabbok. Without an extended pause and some careful pondering, we are likely to place this passage in the category of a one-time special event for special people. Having placed it there, we immediately deny its relevance, disconnect from it and discount its messages for us. As surprising as it may first seem, this passage is resplendent with applicable messages for us. In order to discover them, we need not change the story, only our approach to and interpretation of it. When we get to know him, Jacob is one of us! Could it be that the wrestling match in this story is symbolic of Jacob's life and lifestyle? Even his name fits his character because he is "the grabber." Wrestling was no new experience for him. He had wrestled, in one way or another, for everything he had. Wrestling depicts his past and foreshadows his future. He wrestled from the womb to the tomb. If wrestling was a good teacher, Jacob should have been a smart man. Perhaps he mastered the technique very early in life. That could explain his success when he wrestled with Esau over the birthright and with his father-in-law over the flock.

Could it be that Jacob's wrestling emphasizes an unavoidable day of reckoning? When the core of our being is out of step with God and humanity, we can expect trouble. Literally and figuratively, one can drive the wrong direction in traffic only so long before a wreck occurs. That truth is applicable to our travel on an interstate highway or on the highway of life. Jacob thought he saw the wreck coming, possibly a head on collision with Esau or a rear end collision from hisf ather-in-law, if not both simultaneously. That is a model for any life out of tune with its maker and decent members of society. Unlawful and unholy living may not totally destroy us but it will eventually and certainly put us in serious jeopardy.

The laws of God and humanity are such that we either obey them or get run over by them. Those who disregard them are, possibly unconsciously, asking for a collision. Those who blame God for such difficulty and destruction have placed the blame in the wrong place. Jacob seriously wrestled when he saw the inevitable day of reckoning, not only with his two primary foes but also with God.

Could it be that Jacob wrestled within himself, his own conscience and spirit, as much as with anything else? Entrapment, fear, possibly impending death and a long history of questionable behavior gave him cause to ponder. He was probably alone for the first time in years. Perhaps the night was dark and scary. The wild animals of the night carried on their covert conversations and Jacob had no earthly idea what they meant. He had no control over the unseen creatures and felt helpless in their midst. Perhaps from a distant treetop, he thought the owl called his name. With no herd, no servants and no family nearby, Jacob met Jacob! He recognized what a scoundrel he had been. He knew his two primary enemies were justified in wanting what was theirs, his hide, and possibly his life. The circumstances encouraged him to ponder the meaning of life, his history and his relationship with God. Many of us understand that situation! There were other issues to consider. Jacob was in no hurry to change his behavior because he had previously prospered quite well by it. His underhanded behavior made him financially successful and might eventually have gotten him more wealth than living like his father.

He was an expert in the "grab all you can" system and could follow it in the dark. Did he want to change? Did he have to change? Could he really change? The wrestling match continued! Left alone with his thoughts during that long and lonesome night, he probably recalled the family admonitions given him in his youth. He no doubt recalled the gentle wisdom shared by his aged and religious father. He remembered the special mission to which God had called his family. Jacob may have been overwhelmed when he realized his dad's divine mission came to rest on his own shoulders when he stole the birthright from his brother. Perhaps for the first time, Jacob realized that in that transaction he got what he thought he wanted but now realized he really didn't want what he actually got.

He undoubtedly wrestled with that issue. He understood as never before that deliberate disregard for family values and renouncing divine purposes could not be put permanently out of mind. They lurked in the surrounding shadows and reappeared at the mosti nopportune times. A war raged inside him, between what he was and what he was called to be. He could find no relief until he wrestled with and resolved these issues within his soul.

Could it be this story identifies the difficulty all of us have in ridding ourselves of ingrained and debilitating behavior? Jacob's previous history set the stage for this wrestling match. His lifestyle of trickery and chicanery became imbedded in his being. That is who he was and why he behaved as he did. Jacob was only being Jacob! In order to change his behavior, the core of his being must first be changed. So, it is for everyone. At this point, Jacob was an ordinary person. Our lifestyle inescapably indicates the core of our being out of which we live and move. That is a fundamental fact. We cannot live in the pig pen without smelling like the hogs. If we behave in a certain way long enough, that behavior tells who we are. That is true for positive or negative behavior. Once behavior becomes ingrained in us, it is most difficult to rid ourselves of it. If anyone doubts that, look at your life or talk to a habitual user and abuser of anything that inflicts pain on themselves or others. Behavior tells who we are and it is almost impossible to hide it The wrestling match always continues through the long dark night of our addictions or misdeeds. Wrestling is also an apt description of our normal life. Major or minor choices are not always easy to make. Every decision is crucial because it affects the remainder of our life. We wrestle over the good things, sometimes as much as the "not so good" things. We sometimes wish it were not so but there is no other way.

There are times we wonder who will win. We make a few steps forward but sometimes slide back. Our fiercest foes ambush us when least expected and at our weakest point. They encamp behind and in front of us, hemming us in on all sides. They often possess power to inflict serious pain and to possibly destroy us.

In many other ways, what was true for Jacob is also true for us. Who among us has not fervently sought something by whatever means necessary to get it, only to no longer want it once we got it? It suddenly lost its allurement and gave us additional problems and pain. Is there any among us who has not disregarded sacred admonitions given by parents and religious communities, only to have them suddenly confront us when least expected? The wrestling match continues for us!

Like Jacob, we repeatedly wrestle within our own conscience over a multitude of matters. Our residing evil spirits and our lack of understanding tell us all the good reasons we should not cross over the divide to a new lifestyle. Some of those reasons have a modicum of truth. Some of us wrestle with the idea that we are no good or certainly not good enough to be God's agent for goodness. Some around us may verbalize the same and repeatedly put us down. Jacob reminds us that regardless of what and who we are, we can be converted into something of great value, if our method and motive have God's blessings. We are changed by God's grace, not by our efforts or ability. Our true value lies in what we can become, not in what we have been. Jacob reflects what God can do with us if we cooperate.

Could it be that Jacob did not initially know with whom he wrestled? The story implies that. His opponent was first called a man, then a spirit that could not endure the light of day and finally an angel of God. In all likelihood, that was the progression of his thoughts during the struggle. When he could not overcome the man, himself and his own conscious, he thought he was dealing with an evil spirit. Such spirits were reported to live by ancient streams to forbid strangers from crossing into a "new country."

They also live in us and provide a similar function. Could it be the only evil spirit confronting Jacob was the spirit responsible for his old lifestyle of trickery and deceit? For understandable reasons, it fought to prevent his crossing the divide, "the river," to the side of divinely directed living. That was a new country for Jacob. He had previously lived there in body but not in spirit. That evil spirit in him certainly could not endure the 'light of day", i.e., integrity, honesty, and God's eternal truth.

Jacob didn't want to let the old spirit go, "to cross over," because he must give up a big part of himself. He stubbornly held on. He may not have known how to let it go. He really wrestled over it and with it and agreed to let it go, only if giving it up would provide a blessing for him. And it did! The blessing derived from his old lifestyle came when he realized God could take some parts from that wayward lifestyle and transform them into something constructive and productive. In modern terminology, Jacob did not have to reinvent the wheel but he did have to put it on a new cart which he must use in a vastly different way, from a radically new motive and for a distinctively new purpose. Jacob was not obliterated, just reconfigured and upgraded. In spite of how it first appeared, there was something of value in the old Jacob. His intellectual acumen, ability to see and grab a bargain, and a gift for gab were assets when directed by the proper motive and method.

Could it be that after wrestling with such weighty subjects, Jacob realized these fundamental issues deal with the meaning and purpose
of life itself and part of God's eternal laws? Perhaps Jacob suddenly
saw that life and death, and all in between, were divine matters and nothing is apart from God who truly holds the whole world in his hands. That understanding was a revelatory moment about the eternal nature, purpose and action of God. Jacob now knew who and where God was. Jacob became keenly aware of God's presence with him at that moment. The Hebrew word for "Presence" may also be translated "face to face." Having become acutely cognizant of God's presence with him at that moment, Jacob rightfully described that experience as meeting God face to face. Even when Jacob first thought he was wrestling with a man and then a spirit, he was actually wrestling with God, regardless of the vehicle or form in which God came.

Could it be that during his night of wrestling, Jacob recognized God's willingness to forgive and bestow his grace? God willingly and freely forgave his past and freed him for a productive future, which can only be described as grace. The passage does not specifically state that Jacob reached that conclusion but the situation clearly indicates it. Jacob got what he needed, maybe wanted, but did not deserve. Jacob later met Esau and received Esau's much needed and undeserved forgiveness. Jacob described his meeting Esau with some of the exact words by which he described the wrestling match, saying he saw the face of God in his brother. Esau acted like God by granting forgiveness and grace.

Could it be that the wrestling experience of Jacob foreshadows our own? It depicts the human condition repeatedly experienced by all, to one degree or another. Each of us could spend hours telling how our experiences imitate those of Jacob, from beginning to end. Many of us have spent long, lonesome and sleepless nights in the agonizing darkness of uncertainty. We too have wrestled with life and death situations, knowing that we should or had to do things differently, but unwilling to give up the familiarity of the old for the unknown new.

Change only the name, date, location and a few specifics of Jacob's wrestling match and it parallels the wrestling in our own conscience between what we have done or been and what we know we are called to be and do. We can often replace only his name with our own and see ourselves as actual participants in the story. Therefore, much of what was previously said about Jacob can be truthfully said about us. Perhaps it is wise to reread the story and substitute our name where appropriate.

Jacob's initial uncertainty about his foe reaffirms that he is one of us. It is not uncommon for us to wrestle with something and not be able to precisely identify it. We may be wise enough to know something is amiss in our innards but its name eludes us. We may have to wrestle privately with it just to learn its true name and nature.

However, a thoughtful and honest guess will often help solve the mystery.

We always want our foe to be on the lowest possible level. We intuitively know the smaller the foe the better chance we have to win. In our haste to tilt the match in our favor, we deliberately downgrade our foe and place on it the first and least significant label that comes to mind. Even if the matter is very serious, we tend to say, "Oh, it's really unimportant." That is the normal human procedure, illustrated precisely by Jacob who first identified his opponent as a man. When the wrestling match does not soon cease, we move the label on our foe one notch higher. We attempt to justify our weakness, failure and misdeeds by elevating the power of our foe. We know our odds for winning are radically reduced when we wrestle with some evil spirit embedded in our being. To give that up is to give up a portion of who we are. If it dominated us for quite some time, it is entrenched and fortified. We know its power because previous efforts to rid ourselves of it were unsuccessful. We are bound by our foe and it will not let us go, even if we ask. Deliverance from those evil spirits often require outside help.

The intensity increases over time. Eventually, we declare God, or the gods, are against us. That means serious wrestling is in progress and we fear the outcome.

When resolve and stamina have been pushed to the limits, we know the end of the match is near. At that point in the struggle, it is quite common for us to either give up or gain wisdom. Our wrestling is sometimes made easier when we become wise and admit we may have been incorrect, misinformed or irrational. We realize it is not necessarily God, or the gods, against us but we wrestle because of human failure, either another's or ours. An inner awareness whispers that misinformation and its resulting behavior may be anchored in us. Perhaps the root cause of our confusion was handed down from long ago by customs and people whose issues and circumstances were very different. Being social creatures, we were unavoidably affected by the degree of lameness in our predecessors, as well as their health.

Their crippled minds and customs crippled those who came after them. Because of that and our own weakness and stupidity, we made fools of ourselves, especially when we were lame and did not know it. Since everyone limped, we thought our limping was normal.

Win or lose, we are sometimes seriously wounded or even crippled for life, like Jacob. Serious wrestling may change our behavior by crippling our previous lifestyle, and that can be good. Jacob may have been crippled because he did not know when to quit wrestling. There is a point beyond which wrestling becomes dangerously debilitating. When we wrestle against an unbeatable foe, we eventually become crippled in mind or body, unable to think clearly or to freely and properly perform life's routine activities. The longer we foolishly wrestle the more crippled we become.

An opposite point must be made. If we ceased to wrestle prior to receiving the blessing, a proper or workable resolution, we are crippled in the worst possible way. True wisdom may come only from serious wrestling. Certain attitudes and behaviors facilitate successful wrestling. The primary rules are determined by our ultimate allegiance. A Christian wrestles differently than an atheist and a Methodist wrestles differently than a Mormon. We must first wrestle with knowing for what, when and how long to wrestle! Some things are worth wrestling over and some are not.

Placing certain restraints does not seriously cripple our style but wrestling with no rules resolves nothing. Even if certain limitations apply, we may be better persons after becoming crippled by restraints than without. Being crippled by proper wrestling is a small price to pay for resolving our inner war and having a right relationship with God and others.

Could it be Jacob was crippled in the sense he could no longer haughtily stand in lofty arrogance, proud and erect, answering to no one, as if he were better than others?

For many years and in many ways, he had done that. He was returning to a group of people who knew him for what he was. Therefore, he could no longer fool or take advantage of them. They had his number. In reference to his old behavior, he was crippled and must never again walk that way. He would forever be stooped in spirit, if not in body. In many ways, that properly describes a Christian Could it be that all who serve God are and must forever remain lame to some degree and in a certain sense? A part of our name and nature in this life is and forever will be "lame." We can never remove our human imperfections or our need for God. If we could, we would claim perfection and equality with God, becoming haughty and idolatrous. A genuine and constant awareness of our lameness helps compensate for any limitations it places on us. To be a cripple as the result of joyful obedience to God is to have the greatest possible health and wholeness.

Lameness produced by prolonged wrestling may sometimes be beneficial but it is most often detrimental. Under certain conditions and circumstances, it seemingly provides nothing positive for anyone. Many emotionally scarred people were first wounded in a wrestling match with someone who offered no grace or forgiveness and who were much more powerful than they. All members of any dysfunctional family will limp unless and until an angel of deliverance comes, and possibly thereafter. Abused and abandoned children, all who suffer spousal abuse and malnourishment, misplaced victims of war or famine, those who are oppressed by social conditions, etc., may forever "walk with a limp" because they were basically helpless against other adults and unavoidable circumstances.

Crippled families and crippled people continually pass their malady to others unless an angel of God comes to bless them, but even then, they may have scars. All who are unduly lame announce and propagate their malady by what they say and do, by what is done and left undone. A young female Air Force recruit boldly and unknowingly announced her lameness. She said a female airman would be rapidly promoted in the military if she was willing to "sleep" with a supervisor.

She then proudly proclaimed her desire for promotion! The other crippled and curious males in the group quickly gathered around her, no doubt interested in helping her accomplish her goal! The malady lingers on. The crippling process will continue until we welcome God's angel who comes to deliver us or until we destroy ourselves.

Could it be that Jacob's case of the jitters by the Jabok became the watershed of his life? It was the defining moment for what he was to become. This experience was for him what the Exodus was for the Israelites. Through that experience, he moved from the oldl ife of darkness into the sunrise of a new life. It was a time of revelation, inspiration and deliverance.

The location of Jacob's significant experience deserved an appropriate and special name. He named it "Penuel" or "Peniel" which translates as "The Face of God" or "God's Presence." Those
human words were inadequate to fully describe his experience but they were the best he had and are power-packed with meaning. For him, they identified the place of his transformation. Biblical scholars have not pinpointed its exact location, other than it is east of the Jordan River and in the vicinity of Succoth.

What God did for Jacob long ago, he did or will do for us in an almost identical manner. In the broadest sense, Jacob's conversion is a template of all others. Some particulars may slightly vary but the core experience is always identical. Described by whatever words we choose and located in any place, the bottom line is always the same.

We met God face to face. We confronted his presence in an indescribable way. We became aware that God had given us, even us, undeserved forgiveness and divine grace. That was the watershed of our existence. We became a new being with a new nature and name. By his grace we were forgiven, brought from darkness into light and empowered to become what he called us to be. The "Living Water" washed the mud from us!

Transforming religious experiences make a tremendous impact on a person's life. We, like Jacob, tend to set a marker at that point in our life, either on a specific date or at a particular place. We proudly proclaim the particular place and time it happened, if they can be identified. It may become the experience in our life by which all others are dated, either before or after that blessing. The small country church of our youth, the youth camp, the camp meeting, the revival meeting, the magnificent cathedral, etc., are not easily forgotten, nor should they be. "Meeting God face to face" and knowing we too have received undeserved grace and forgiveness are no trivial matters. It is certainly worthy of an appropriate celebration, a marker and a descriptive name. Periodic returns to that place may renew the memory and revive the awareness of its significance.

Could it be that Jacob was greatly surprised after he wrestled with God, met him face to face, and won? If he was, behind that surprise lay the old assumption that no mortal can survive close proximity to God and certainly not if one met him face to face. Given his previous understanding of God, Jacob was very surprised to discover God's nature was far different than he assumed. The legalistic emphasis of his forefathers was replaced with an emphasis on grace. The God of Grace is not situated on some distant mountain or in some specific isolated and holy place. The God of Grace comes to us where we are, even wrestles with us and for us. We are not destroyed when we meet him face to face. Instead, that is the process through which and by which we find new life.

Had Jacob initially known it was God with whom he wrestled, he probably would have immediately given up. After the wrestling match, Jacob knew why and what he won. To say he won, does not mean he had overpowered God and forced God to do what God did not intend to do. It means Jacob got the best possible results he could get out of it. God had given him far more than he could ask for or expect, and especially more than he could ever give God. God remained the same but Jacob was transformed. He won because he experienced God's transforming grace.

Could it be that our wrestling matches with God are always designed so that we can win? Our wrestling with God will never overpower him or redesign his nature but it holds the only possibility for us to have our nature and will properly transformed through God's grace. Perhaps wrestling with matters of life and death is the normal process through which we discover who God is and how he works. Could it be that the secret to a meaningful life is not avoiding wrestling matches but rather a readiness to wrestle?

Like Jacob, we must hold on to the angel of mercy until the blessing comes because there may be no other angel and no other chance for deliverance. When we meet God face to face on a particular issue, we win if we become better than we were, regardless of the medium through which it came. God never wrestles with anything that is unimportant to him! Therefore, every wrestling match with God is one more firm indication of our worth and his grace. The outcome of every wrestling match is announced by whether or not the wrestler receives a new name and/or a new nature. Deliverance is declared when we, like Jacob, get a new name and a new identity. A new name announces a distinct change in the one who receives it. "Jacob, the grabber" or "the heel" became "Israel, the Prince of God." In keeping with ancient customs, his new name conveyed a specific message when spoken.

Our new name is similar and also conveys a distinct message when spoken. It signifies a new being, new behavior and a new beginning. "Christian" is our new name and love is our new nature.

Having been transformed by wrestling with God, we are no longer 'godless" but "godly," no longer "without Christ" but "Christian," no longer an "addict" but a "recovering addict," no longer an "abuser of others" but a "friend," etc. We can be absolutely sure others will soon know our new name and nature. Someone correctly said it long ago, "They will know we are Christians by our love." Even though this passage first seems to be about Jacob, it is also about us. It relates a story about a special person in a special place under special conditions but it tells far more than that. It is also a story for us and about us.

It reminds us that Jacob's God is our God and he is the same yesterday, today and forever. Therefore, he continues to wrestle with us and we with him so that he might bless us with his grace. We have the option to receive it or renounce it. We may often wrestle with him and not know it is he. If we are absolutely honest, we will sometimes say it is with others, with our conscience, with all sorts of evil spirits and with God. Perhaps we would be wiser still to realize that, in the final analysis, every worthwhile wrestling match is always with God.

CHAPTER SIX
Asking For Too Much
Exodus 33:18-23

18: Moses said, "I pray thee, show me thy glory."

19: And he said, "I will make all my goodness pass before you, and will proclaim before you my name "The LORD"; and I will be gracious to whom I will be gracious, and will show mercy on whom I will show mercy.

20: But," he said, "you cannot see my face; for man shall not see me and live."

21: And the LORD said, "Behold, there is a place by me where you shall stand upon the rock;

22: and while my glory passes by I will put you in a cleft of the rock, and I will cover you with my hand until I have passed by;

23: then I will take away my hand, and you shall see my back; but my face shall not be seen."

The followers of Moses could not stay out of trouble. In the passages of scripture preceding the one mentioned above, Moses returned from visiting God on the sacred mountain with two stone tablets containing the original version of the God-given Ten Commandments tucked under his arm. To his great consternation, Moses found his followers reveling in a pagan party, centered on an idol they formed with their own hands from gold they brought with them from Egypt. In anger, Moses flung down the stones and broke them. All that Moses said may not be recorded in the scripture!!!

God and Moses were not pleased with the pagan party in the Israelite's camp. As an indication of his deep displeasure, God informed Moses he was withdrawing his divine presence from

Moses' followers. In fact, God was so mad with them he said he would destroy them if he came among them. Needless to say, Moses did not like what he saw or heard so he sought to change God's mind. Moses knew how he and his followers got where they were and he also knew God's presence among them was their only source of hope for getting where they needed to go.

Given the rebellious behavior of the Israelites, God and Moses debated to whom those practicing pagans rightfully belonged. Apparently, God was disgusted with the whole bunch and decided to give up on then. God said they belonged to Moses. Moses reminded God that they were his because God personally delivered them from Egypt and gave them a particular promise. During the conversation, the story indicates God began to mellow. Sensing new possibilities, Moses pled with God for some specific things. God granted a portion of Moses' request but not everything. Moses asked for too much.

This is another biblical passage easily relegated to the category of "special action for special people under special circumstances" that has little or nothing to do with us in the here and now. After all, who among us has ever seen God or had a face to face conversation with him? Who among us can correctly declare, "This is what God said to me?" Who among us believes anyone who reports they had a direct message from God? Having had no experiences remotely similar to those of Moses, we most often pronounce this biblical passage irrelevant and send it to the religious scrap heap.

If we desire a better understanding of God's revelation of himself, a casual and swift dismissal of this passage is definitely unwise. Once again, we need not rewrite the passage to find its message. We need only to interpret it from a new direction. Tucked away in the corners of this strange story are fundamental principles for life and deep theological truths that are as relevant today as they were in the day of Moses. These eternal truths and principles must be forever remembered or else we too will likely participate in a pagan party, perhaps without knowing it. This story is also for us.

Could it be this passage deals with an ageless question confronting biblical writers and us? This and adjoining passages unquestionably raise the issue of whether or not mortals can cause God to change a decision he has made, or change his mind. That subject has been, and will be, debated for many years. When the debate ceases, we mortals will not yet have the final answer. We can only ponder and surmise. If we ask God for the ability to fully answer that question, we have, like Moses, asked for too much.

All of us have our opinions on the matter but we must realize our answers are only partial, at best. Any approach we take or partial answer we offer depends heavily on other personal beliefs and theological assumptions. Chief among them is our understanding of the will of God. The matter of God changing his mind is more correctly stated as God changing his will.

Numerous religious scholars have sorted through some possibilities for better understanding God's will and have given us a framework within which to speak intelligently about it. Their recorded thoughts are sometimes helpful but not final. This is not the place to summarize what they said or argue the pros and cons of their comments.
Could it be that God's will have always been and shall always be exactly as it presently is? From what we have seen and from what we now understand, that seems more logical and makes more sense than to assume he was, or is, indecisive and can be swayed by his subjects. If God is the same yesterday, today and forever, a willingness to change, for whatever reason, would seemingly negate that fact.

Could it be that God's will is somewhat like an extensive and intricate mathematical equation not yet fully known to us but partially understood? In an effort to solve it, we make use of what we already know about other equations and pay particular attention to its relationship to them. Maybe God's will is somewhat like the DNA blueprint for the human body which we have not yet completely unraveled. Even there, we use what we now know in order to discover the unknown. The format of the equation and the DNA structure are set in stone.

Change, disregard or delete any part and the full potential will be destroyed and the desired results will be denied. In order to get a fuller understanding, it must be accepted and followed as it is.

If God's will is somewhat similar to that, other comments are in order. We do not have the complete formula or an exact model to fully understand God's will. Its fullness is a mystery. We only have some significant clues to it. Therefore, we carefully work with what we understand and we diligently seek to know as much as is humanly possible. It is certainly advisable for us to communicate with and learn from others who pursue the same quest. The difficulty of our quest emphasizes the urgency for people, like Moses, to seek God's will above all else. Since it is impossible to fully understand it, how shall we discover more than we already know? The scripture passage mentioned above provides excellent insight.

Could it be wise to say humanity progressively changed its understanding of God's will, beginning with creation and continuing to the present? If that basically describes what happened, we have an understandable explanation for diverse and divergent interpretations of it for particular people in particular places. However, a specific or commonly accepted interpretation does not necessarily mean it was or is correct. Some things originally attributed to the will of God may later be labeled differently.

Could it be that Moses' recorded conversation with God in this passage is more correctly described as wrestling to discover God's will for that time, place and group of people? Never let it be said that God did not or cannot verbally converse with mortals. However, none of us have ever experienced that and we have no reputable report of anyone who has been so blessed. On the other hand, many of us can relate personal experiences when we wrestled with some issue, seeking to discern God's will in reference to it. Some of us had an experience through which we discovered an answer we believed was sent from God. If that is what really took place in this story, then Moses is a mortal like us, struggling to ascertain God's will. That fact alone makes the story very relevant.

Moses was no dummy. He diligently sought to know God's will. Many years and countless hours of deep meditation, serious concentration and genuine worship of God gave him insights not known by others. Quiet contemplation and careful evaluation contributed greatly toward understanding God's will for his particular situation. Moses' heart, mind and character were of a godly nature. Apparently, he diligently sought to remain in tune with God's will.

He was saturated with an awareness of the presence of God. Based on what he had seen and experienced, he felt sure God had blessed him in a special way and with special answers.

Could it be that Moses fully believed God had given him guidance for their journey, the Commandments, insights, warnings, messages, etc.? Moses would never claim ownership or authorship of such magnificent revelations. Therefore, he could describe all words and insights that came to him with no other verbiage than "God said...." God had "said it" because it came to him as a gift from God. After all he had experienced, Moses did not have to audibly hear God's voice to recognize God's message

Could it be this is an analogy of how God speaks to us today? After extensive prayer, meditation, study and worship, we discover what we fully believe is his will. It is a temporary understanding, one we follow until another is granted. We must never make the erroneous assumption that we have finally accomplished our goal. We must continue our close relationship with God so that we may receive any new revelation if and when it is offered. If we are convinced our insight was granted by God, we correctly describe it by saying, "God spoke to me." Even though we did not actually hear his voice, we were certain we discovered his will. It came to us from him. However, if we are convinced it came, it usually arrived only after we consciously and seriously sought it. We then proclaim it with hesitancy and humility.

Religious leaders have a responsibility to help others discover God's will. Having "heard" God, as described above, they also have a message from God for those under their leadership.

If some things are true for the leader, then similar things are most likely applicable to the followers. A leader informs others. However, a genuine spiritual leader always recognizes the possibility for personal error and reminds followers of their fallibility. That leader will also remind others of a personal responsibility to ascertain God's will, remembering they too may be mistaken. Genuine leaders, as well as followers, are also held accountable when they proclaim ani nappropriate message. Could it be Moses never made any attempt to change God's mind? Moses was too smart for that. Though never said but repeatedly implied throughout this passage, Moses expressed a willingness and desire to change his own mind and heart so that he could maintain a close relationship with God. Moses seemed sure he had a special relationship and even spoke of having found favor with God who knew him by name.

Arguing with God could have easily moved Moses out of his favored relationship, especially if he pressured God to change the divine rules. Moses knew you "Don't mess with God."

Could it be Moses struggled to maintain his special relationship with God because associating with the wayward and sometimes pagan Israelites came close to severing it? They distracted him from the divine purpose and tempted him to give up the mission to which he was called. Their repeated disobedience and disregard for God made him wonder if they would ever fulfill God's mission for and promise to them. His laborious efforts to get them back on track and to solve their petty problems robbed him of his much-needed time to ponder and pray. Their disobedience and disregard for God tempted him to do ungodly things. Moses knew if he lost that relationship with God, he could not endure the pressure of leadership and there would be no need for them to go anywhere. If God's activity in their midst ceased, Moses and the Israelites were doomed. Their only hope was a conscious and positive response to God whose active presence separated them from others and made them a distinct people.

Could it be this is an urgent message for each of us, for every American and for all people in the world? From the Judeo-Christian perspective, that which makes us distinctive is the awareness of God's presence among us and our conscious positive response to it. If we lose that awareness and make no conscious effort to respond positively, we are in serious trouble and there is little or nothing to separate us from other pagans. Having become disconnected from God in thought and deed, we worship idols of our own creation, just like the wayward Israelites.

Human behavior may be no more godless now than it has ever been but there are indications of serious danger ahead, if we are not already experiencing it. The warnings of this passage are applicable to us.
Could it be that Moses made a mistake common to all who believe they have a special relationship with God? Having confidence, he had found favor with God and a promise of perpetual presence, Moses decided to see what else he could get. Moses was human after all! A human tendency is to test the limits, to see how far we can go before we are forced to stop.

That behavior is demonstrated every day in thousands of ways, both around and in us. It may not be necessarily bad but it is deeply dangerous if we do not deliberately keep it under control. As a note of interest, even Jesus confronted that temptation. For reasons known only to him, Moses asked God to reveal his "Glory." We are not sure for what Moses asked because the word "Glory" has various meanings. It could mean he wanted complete understanding of God and undeniable proof of God's presence with him. All of us can understand his desire. If Moses had traveled by sincere faith to this physical and spiritual point in his life, asking for proof that God would continually be with him made good sense to him. Perhaps he said, "Give me some definite answers, God. Let mei n on the plan." "Glory" is sometimes used to speak of God's wrath that rains down on those who disobeyed him. It is easy to see how Moses was thoroughly disgusted with his followers and wanted God to severely punish them for their disobedience. Moses undoubtedly believed they should be made acutely aware of the fact God does not tolerate or leave unpunished such sinful behavior.

Perhaps Moses fully accepted the adage, "Spare the rod and spoil the child" or maybe he coined it! It is only human to want others punished for their misdeeds, in hopes the punishment will deter further failure, especially if you are partially responsible for them.

"Glory" may also mean "Presence" or "fullness of God" or "God's total self." Moses wanted to meet God face to face, to see and completely understand him as he is. He may have asked God for a full and complete disclosure of his character, nature and will, leaving nothing to be discovered through agonizing meditation, prayer, study, worship and faith. Moses wanted the correct answers without hard work and possible errors.

"Glory" may mean "purpose." It is only human and highly understandable that Moses wanted to know God's purpose for all he had endured and for all that was to come. Moses may have been tired, physically and emotionally.

Those grumbling and wayward Israelites had taken the spring out of his step and the excitement out of the journey. If only he knew the purpose and final outcome, he could faithfully endure all future struggles. Without that information, perhaps he feared he might lose sight of his own purpose and promise. Moses wanted to know all there was to know about God. For whatever he asked, it was too much because mortals can never know everything about God. God knew better than to fully grant the request. The struggle to know may have been the very thing that kept Moses faithful and a vivid reminder of his humanity.

We also know only what God chooses to reveal but the amount of revelation is probably in direct proportion to our ability and struggle to know. The struggle for additional insight may be the very thing that keeps us faithful and it is our constant and necessary reminder that we are only human. The struggle is persistent and permanent. In order to know all there is to know about God, one must be equal to or bigger than God. No mortal can correctly claim such knowledge. If they had it, they would no longer be human.

Following his agonizing search and unwise request, Moses no doubt knew he wanted what he could not have. That is a common human desire known by most of us. We can even give wonderful reasons why we should have it and dream of how much we could do with it. We are no different than Moses at that point. The passage gently chastises Moses with a new revelation, reminding him God does what God chooses to do and for whom he chooses, without the awareness, knowledge or permission of Moses. So, it is with us!

Could it be that we should give special attention to God's response to Moses' request for what he could not have? Too many among us have not accepted the chastisement nor do they believe there is anything about God or his will that they do not already know. Uneducated country preachers, TV evangelists, late night radio preachers and self-appointed religious leaders tend to disregard the discovery of Moses. They are definitely not the only ones and even some of them are true messengers of God.

God's response to Moses reminds us that those who claim a special knowledge of God may be very far away from where they think they are, or maybe it is where they want us to think they are! Those who assume knowledge that only God possesses do far more harm than good. Within a short time, they can easily and instantly inflict more damage to the Judeo-Christian cause than others can ever repair. They may light the fire in which an idol is formed but most of them keep the gold for themselves! Some seek the exact description of heaven, who will go there, how many, etc. They ask for a precise definition of sin and a list of "dos and don'ts" that guarantee them a ticket to heaven. They want a checklist by which to determine who is or is not right with God. They demand the exact date for the end of time and the precise signs of its coming. Their request for absolute certainty goes on and on. According to the answer that came to Moses, they ask for too much. Even though no mortal has that knowledge, that is no deterrent for false prophets who worship the idols of wealth, power, popularity, etc.

Absolute answers are intriguing but they would destroy our humanity. All dispensers of proposed absolute answers, and all who spend an inordinate amount of time diligently seeking them, should ponder the story where Moses asked for too much. The answer to Moses is also our answer. Some matters are beyond our understanding and only God holds the answer. Anyone who thinks they must have absolute answers has not yet learned to live by faith in the goodness, power and mercy of God. Perhaps without knowing it, they come close to claiming equality with God and pretend to possess knowledge known only to him. That is idolatry. They are like the wayward Israelites who, in the heat of their selfish desires, formed an idol made from what they already possessed. Perhaps such behavior is best described as making an idol from what possessed them.

If we do not and cannot ever fully know or understand God's will, what shall we do? Let us have faith and rejoice. We can know enough to fulfill his call and command to us. God is always ready to reveal as much of his nature and will as we are able to endure.

Could it be that is precisely the meaning of Ex. 33:19b, indicating God will be gracious and show mercy to whomever he chooses?

The closing verses of our passage provide unique insight to Moses and are tremendously valuable to us. The location and verbiage of the last verse provide a forceful and partial summation of what has already been said but adds what is frequently forgotten, if not totally overlooked. We only see the "back side" of God because we can never fully understand him.

If God chastised Moses because he asked for too much, God was not angry with Moses for asking. In essence, God said, "Even though I cannot give you everything for which you asked because it will destroy you, I will give you some guidance to discover who I am and how I act." God offered a compromise.

God's glory, his total being, would pass by, or be present, but Moses would not and could not see (understand) all of it. Symbolically, the story makes that point when Moses crouched in a crack between the rocks and God shaded Moses' eyes. God's "glory" passed by but Moses was allowed to see God's "back," but not his "face." Moses could endure the sight of where God had been, "his back," but could never know everything about God or where God was going. Moses could recognize God's previous action but he was not privileged to predict God's future activity.

The closing verses indicate Moses inappropriately pursued his quest. He originally wanted full knowledge of God's nature and intended activity. If granted, that would destroy the humanity of Moses. Since he was and would remain human, he saw only the "back of God" and it would always be that way. He must remain God's servant, not his equal.

Could it be that new insight comes not by attempting to ascertain where God is going but by recognizing where God has been, what God has done and how he apparently did it? God always leaves his footprints and shadow when he passes. We can never perfectly predict where God is going but, with proper effort, we can be reasonably sure he went by. From what we already know and from the clues left behind, we have enough to guide and sustain us on our religious journey.

Faithful religious discipline provides new revelation when we need it most and when it pleases God.

Could it be that these closing verses give us what we need to know and that for which we have longed, namely genuine insight into how God reveals himself? Perhaps this is the primary purpose for the passage? Since we are human, the complete revelation of God is beyond our understanding and God will never grant it to us, regardless of how religious we are or how much we beg. God does for us the best he can, given our human capacity and his will. Like Moses, we are incapable of seeing him in his fullness.

We are able to see only his "back" but that gives us some strong indications of who he is, how he acts and what he requires. That may be all of God we can tolerate without being destroyed in some manner. He reveals only what we can endure.

Could it be this passage provides a clue for pondering the revelations given by Christ? Since God reveals only what we can endure, it follows that Jesus revealed only the part of God that would not destroy our humanity. Even though God was in Christ, there is more of God than we are able to see in Christ. Likewise, the early Christians understood much more about the mission and ministry of Jesus after he departed than when he was present. "They saw his back." They learned the most from his "footprints" and "shadow." In terms of our scripture passage, they did not fully recognize him when face to face but they did recognize him after he passed by.

Could it be this passage also says we are never able to look upon an approaching event, look it full in the face, and rightfully declare it is or is not the will of God? However, after it passes, we are able to reasonably judge, based upon its footprints and prior revelations.

Perhaps we must measure everything by the shadowy evidence of God that is all around us. In passing, and by his presence, God provided clues by which to make a reasonable judgment about his eternal will and way. Those clues are not always seen or interpreted the same by everyone. No single event stands alone but must always be judged in light of what was previously deduced from former situations and experiences. We must ask, "Does it fit with what we have previously and carefully concluded or does it offer something new?" It becomes more urgent for us to maintain a proper relationship with God through prayer, meditation, study, worship and religious fellowship. Therein lies our best hope in discerning God's will. Even after we have diligently searched for the answer, we must always remember our humanity. We can never be absolutely sure our judgment is correct but we can be absolutely sure it is the best we have at the moment and we will abide by it until, by a revelation from God, we learn better.

If we have faithfully and correctly followed God's footprints and rightfully read the clues, his will has always been and shall forever be inescapably associated with love. His nature and his character are best described as love. Even when we ask for too much, seek improper things and erect our idols, he continues to love us and calls us to love him and one another.

God will not change his mind or our basic human nature. Stubborn disobedience, worshipping idols, demanding or claiming inappropriate knowledge, etc., may cause God to "weep" over our stupidity but it does not change his will. Living the most God-like life possible will not cause God to give us information that is "for his eyes only." Our disobedience, or obedience, does not change his will. That would mean he is subservient to us and we would be more powerful than God.

Though strange and somewhat difficult to understand, this passage has superb value for all who ponder God's will and ask whether or not he changes his mind? This response to the above-mentioned scripture is not the final answer. At best, it is only partial and temporary. Hopefully, it will assist us in finding a more meaningful answer and a new revelation that keeps us from asking for too much.

CHAPTER SEVEN
Falling Off His High Horse
Acts 9:1-19

1: But Saul, still breathing threats and murder against the disciples of the Lord, went to the high priest

2: and asked him for letters to the synagogues at Damascus, so that if he found any belonging to the Way, men or women, he might bring them bound to Jerusalem.

3: Now as he journeyed, he approached Damascus, and suddenly a light from heaven flashed about him.

4: And he fell to the ground and heard a voice saying to him, "Saul, Saul, why do you persecute me?"

5: And he said, "Who are you, Lord?" And he said, "I am Jesus, whom you are persecuting;

6: but rise and enter the city, and you will be told what you are to do."

7: The men who were traveling with him stood speechless, hearing the voice but seeing no one.

8: Saul arose from the ground; and when his eyes were opened, he could see nothing; so, they led him by the hand and brought him into Damascus.

9: And for three days he was without sight, and neither ate nor drank.

10: Now there was a disciple at Damascus named Anani'as. The Lord said to him in a vision, "Anani'as." And he said, "Here I am, Lord."

11: And the Lord said to him, "Rise and go to the street called Straight, and inquire in the house of Judas for a man of Tarsus named Saul; for behold, he is praying,

12: and he has seen a man named Anani'as come in and lay his hands on him so that he might regain his sight."

13: But Anani'as answered, "Lord, I have heard from many about this man, how much evil he has done to thy saints at Jerusalem;

14: and here he has authority from the chief priests to bind all who call upon thy name."

15: But the Lord said to him, "Go, for he is a chosen instrument of mine to carry my name before the Gentiles and kings and the sons of Israel;

16: for I will show him how much he must suffer for the sake of my name."

17: So Anani'as departed and entered the house. And laying his hands on him he said, "Brother Saul, the Lord Jesus who appeared to you on the road by which you came, has sent me that you may regain your sight and be filled with the Holy Spirit."

18: And immediately something like scales fell from his eyes and he regained his sight. Then he rose and was baptized,

19: and took food and was strengthened. For several days he was with the disciples at Damascus.

Was Saul of Tarsus, later known as Paul, knocked from his horse during his conversion experience? Sermons, Sunday school teachers, fervent Christians and artists often indicate he was.

In addition to the above-mentioned passage about Paul's conversion, two other accounts are found; Acts 22:616 and 26:12-18. Each passage gives a slightly different account. It matters not which one you prefer or what you previously thought, there is no specific or implied reference to a horse in either. If a horse is in this story, the reader led it there!

All three passages agree that Paul, and perhaps all others with him, "fell to the ground" but do not clearly indicate from where he or they fell.

Even though we have some specific details of Paul's conversion, we do not know precisely what happened. We only know what the stories report. Based on the results, something strange and powerful undoubtedly occurred. Whatever it was, Paul's life was radically transformed by it.

We have no reason to question the sequence of reported events but they do not give us the whole story. Gaps remain and we tend to fill them with our own imagination or with erroneous information gleaned from others, such as putting a horse in the story. We want all the intricate details and tend to manufacture them if they are absent. Anyone who provides more details than contained in the story should be seriously questioned about their source.

Some will argue Paul fell from a horse because that was the primary method of travel for prominent people in his day. Others argue he was walking, since most everyone traveled over land on foot in those days. One may choose to argue for either method of travel but this story provides no information on Paul's mode of travel. Records tell us he later sailed to certain destinations but we can be quite sure he was not traveling by boat on the road to Damascus.

This story reports at least five extraordinary things that cause some modern readers to seriously question its relevance. First, Paul was literally knocked to the ground by an unidentified and unseen force. Second, he was totally blinded by a mysterious and intense light.

Third, he later regained his sight only after something similar to scales fell from his eyes. Fourth, he actually heard God speak. Fifth, a fearful stranger who had not witnessed the event made special effort to find Paul and to converse with him about his experience. Without further explanation and insight, these five factors tend to identify this story as another "one-time event for a special person under specific circumstances."

Those elements in Paul's conversion story extend far beyond our personal experiences. In its present form, most average readers find no handles to grasp its significance and no obvious point for personal connection. Since it is incomplete and some well-meaning religious people frequently misinterpret it, skeptics tend to disregard it. Given these facts, it can easily be considered another somewhat informative but irrelevant biblical story easily relegated to the religious scrap heap. Could it be that we do a disservice to ourselves, and the passage, if we quickly send it to the religious garbage dump? Encompassed in this unusual story are some essential lessons for our own religious edification. In order to find them, we do not have to rewrite the story or disregard portions of it in order to make it relevant. We need only to interpret it from a different perspective.

Could it be that one reason for our inclination to declare it irrelevant is an unconscious and uncomfortable response to it? It is not a story that makes us feel good when we read or hear it. For some reason, it agitates our innards. Many modern religious proclamations are purposely designed to make us feel good. Our society most often values something on the basis of whether or not it makes us feel good. This story fails that test so it may be quickly discarded.

Could it be we are afraid to remain immobile long enough for serious contemplation of this story because the same spirit that confronted Paul might suddenly confront us? "Spirit" is not a hot topic where we live. Our insistence on excessive activity and constant noise keep us from considering more serious matters of life. Perpetual motion and strict adherence to an agenda, ours or another's, destroy any opportunity to ponder religious matters.

Such behavior is not always accidental. In our scientific and sophisticated age, the quiet pondering of serious and sacred matters is taboo and too old fashioned for those who are "really with it." We not only refuse to talk about them with others but we are also reluctant to even think about such matters.

Could it be we purposely disregard this passage, not because we think it is irrelevant but primarily because we fear it is extremely relevant? Our inner voice whispers that religious matters are serious business and we have some unfinished business in that regard.

Are we afraid to ponder it because it may disturb our personal status quo? A vague awareness of what happened to Paul during and following that experience discourages our desire for something as radical to happen to us. Many of us profess a firm belief in religion, but not the kind that totally changes our lives and makes us do weird things. How would we explain a radical change to our family? What would our friends think? If extensive change makes us very uncomfortable, we usually seek to preserve our status quo at all cost. Fervent and frequent denial of its relevance delays having to deal with it.

Could it be some of us who claim to be Christian shun this passage because it produces probing and personal questions about our own conversion? For several reasons, we may wonder if what we experienced was the real thing. Some deeply religious folk repeatedly told us we had no conversion unless it was as cataclysmic and instantaneous as Paul's. They declare one must be able to give the precise date, exact time and specific location or it has not happened. Some of us don't have that and are bothered over not having it. We ask, "What if they are correct?"

Some who demand such specifics are widely known in religious circles and are accepted as religious authorities. Even if we strongly disagree, we have no desire to make a fool of ourselves arguing with someone of such prominence, especially if we are unsure of what God requires and lack the ability or knowledge to defend our personal view. It is simpler and less uncomfortable to avoid the issue.

Even though many argue that a valid conversion must be almost identical to Paul's, their argument is usually based on the erroneous assumption that all religious conversions must be instantaneous and cataclysmic. Those two terms are not applicable to all genuine religious conversions, regardless of what a renowned preacher, television evangelist or well-meaning pastor would have us believe.

Conversions described with those words are often not as instantaneous as first thought. The exact manner through which they came, the length of time over which they came, the exact moment they came and the degree of change wrought by them are seldom known and have nothing to do with the genuineness of conversion experiences. A specific time, date and place is undoubtedly comforting and meaningful for anyone who can correctly give them. However, they are not absolutely necessary. An insistence upon being able to give that information may be unchristian! It sounds as if we can determine the conditions for a conversion and judge its validity. It also fails to recognize the vast diversity in God's design. Furthermore, just because specific facts were stated, that is no guaranty it happened.

Quiet, steady and minor changes also make permanent impressions. No majestic oak reached its stature through a cataclysmic and instantaneous process. The constant dripping of water over an extended period erodes a rock. Our conversion may come to us like the oak's stature or the rock's erosion. It may come slowly, steadily, almost unnoticed and over a long time. God apparently performs a majority of his wonderful deeds over an extended period, certainly not always instantaneously. If God successfully moves slowly in many other areas, it would be extremely strange that he is unable to slowly effect a conversion in us? One size does not fit all! Therefore, we need not shun the passage just because our conversion was not an exact replica of Paul's. Could it be that Paul's conversion was not instantaneous? His awareness of it may have been instant but even that is doubtful. Radical change seldom, if ever, happens instantly. Numerous factors had been at work on Paul for a long time.

He probably knew that and it helps explain why he journeyed toward Damascus "breathing threats and murder against the disciples." His vicious vendetta illustrated an inner struggle. His previous interactions with numerous Christians had a disturbing effect on him and he didn't like it. The witness and response of Stephen and others, in whose death and misery Paul participated, progressively left their marks on Paul. The spirit and faith of those Christians whom he sought to silence gradually eroded his egotistical armor. Their unwavering trust in God

Are we afraid to ponder it because it may disturb our personal status quo? A vague awareness of what happened to Paul during and following that experience discourages our desire for something as radical to happen to us. Many of us profess a firm belief in religion, but not the kind that totally changes our lives and makes us do weird things. How would we explain a radical change to our family? What would our friends think? If extensive change makes us very uncomfortable, we usually seek to preserve our status quo at all cost. Fervent and frequent denial of its relevance delays having to deal with it.

Could it be some of us who claim to be Christian shun this passage because it produces probing and personal questions about our own conversion? For several reasons, we may wonder if what we experienced was the real thing. Some deeply religious folk repeatedly told us we had no conversion unless it was as cataclysmic and instantaneous as Paul's. They declare one must be able to give the precise date, exact time and specific location or it has not happened. Some of us don't have that and are bothered over not having it. We ask, "What if they are correct?"

Some who demand such specifics are widely known in religious circles and are accepted as religious authorities. Even if we strongly disagree, we have no desire to make a fool of ourselves arguing with someone of such prominence, especially if we are unsure of what God requires and lack the ability or knowledge to defend our personal view. It is simpler and less uncomfortable to avoid thei ssue.

Even though many argue that a valid conversion must be almost identical to Paul's, their argument is usually based on the erroneous assumption that all religious conversions must be instantaneous and cataclysmic. Those two terms are not applicable to all genuine religious conversions, regardless of what a renowned preacher, television evangelist or well-meaning pastor would have us believe.

Conversions described with those words are often not as instantaneous as first thought. The exact manner through which they came, the length of time over which they came, the exact moment they came and the degree of change wrought by them are seldom known and have nothing to do with the genuineness of conversion experiences. A specific time, date and place is undoubtedly comforting and meaningful for anyone who can correctly give them. However, they are not absolutely necessary. An insistence upon being able to give that information may be unchristian! It sounds as if we can determine the conditions for a conversion and judge its validity. It also fails to recognize the vast diversity in God's design. Furthermore, just because specific facts were stated, that is no guaranty it happened. Quiet, steady and minor changes also make permanent impressions. No majestic oak reached its stature through a cataclysmic and instantaneous process. The constant dripping of water over an extended period erodes a rock. Our conversion may come to us like the oak's stature or the rock's erosion. It may come slowly, steadily, almost unnoticed and over a long time. God apparently performs a majority of his wonderful deeds over an extended period, certainly not always instantaneously. If God successfully moves slowly in many other areas, it would be extremely strange that he is unable to slowly effect a conversion in us? One size does not fit all! Therefore, we need not shun the passage just because our conversion was not an exact replica of Paul's.

Could it be that Paul's conversion was not instantaneous? His awareness of it may have been instant but even that is doubtful. Radical change seldom, if ever, happens instantly. Numerous factors had been at work on Paul for a long time. He probably knew that and it helps explain why he journeyed toward Damascus "breathing threats and murder against the disciples."

His vicious vendetta illustrated an inner struggle. His previous interactions with numerous Christians had a disturbing effect on him and he didn't like it. The witness and response of Stephen and others, in whose death and misery Paul participated, progressively left their marks on Paul. The spirit and faith of those Christians whom he sought to silence gradually eroded his egotistical armor. Their unwavering trust in God and their inner peace repeatedly haunted Paul's troubled soul. A deep commitment to specifically selected scripture and religious laws stood in opposition to what he witnessed among the Christians. That contradiction no doubt gnawed at his innards.

His fervent attempt to silence the Christians was only another indication of his own spiritual unrest. At the initial reading of this story, Paul's conversion appears to have been instantaneous and it is the type coveted and claimed by many modern Christians. That type is a wonderful life-changing experience for those who needed it and believe they had it. When interpreted emotionally, that description is understandable, but when interpreted rationally, it is rather unlikely a radical transformation occurred instantaneously.

Without doubt, the gradual, quiet and extended influence of others effected change in Paul. Eventually, the culminating effects of those influences suddenly broke into his awareness. Some call that sudden awareness instantaneous and cataclysmic. The culmination of the process may have been instantaneously recognized but the process encompassed many days and diverse events. Modern conversions are no different.

Recognition that something wonderful happened may be sudden but seldom is it a complete surprise. Even with instant realization and recognition that radical change is necessary or has come, that too may have been quietly growing for a long time, during doubts, indecision and dissatisfaction, not during times of perfect inner peace. Having reached a sudden awareness, it is quite common for everyone to look back and identify factors contributing to the experience. God works in his own way and according to his own time. Who among us dare dictate how he must do it?

Paul's conscious surrender may have been instantaneous but his religious alterations were not. The "instantaneous event" on the Damascus road was surely a culmination of known and unknown influences, some of which he might be able to identify at a later time. Following the experience, Paul fervently sought to learn and understand its meaning. He may have been instantly aware that something happened but it took him a long time to fully decipher its ramification. In fact, he appears to have been in a daze immediately after it. In the days and years that followed, he often adjusted his life in keeping with new insights.

Could it be this is the normal transformation process for every religious conversion, regardless of its dimensions, description and required time? Various influences do God's work until the necessity for change is consciously acknowledged, sometimes instantly and sometimes over an unknown period of time.

Some change may occur instantly but much of it will come over time because it seems humanly impossible for every required change to be instantly realized and finalized. Like Paul, we may find it helpful, if not necessary, to consult with others in order to make the proper alterations and understand their full meaning. Change is more of a process than an instant event since one alteration often necessitates another, some of which may be minuscule and others may be major.

Could it be that much of our difficulty with this passage and our arguments about religious conversions, come from one basic source? Perhaps we lack agreement on what constitutes a valid religious conversion. Simply stated, "conversion" means change. At its most fundamental level, any change is a conversion of some sort. Following it, something is no longer as it previously was. The degree of change and the time required for it are not important at this point. Generally speaking, change may or may not have a religious flavor. Any personal change with a religious flavor can be correctly called a religious conversion. As we all know, some conversions make a radical difference in a person's life while others are hardly noticeable.

By definition, each is a genuine conversion and will be reflected in the behavior of the one to whom it came. Any attempt to further describe or define a religious conversion experience is dangerous business because we are speaking of divine action and human response. Precise definition of the experience limits it. God is not limited by our definition. Unless we are extremely careful, every attempt to precisely define it will be based on the definer's experience and some preconceived personal ideas. How presumptuous of someone to assume they are able to define how God effects a change in anyone. How idolatrous to assume we can tell God how he must do the deed. None among us can rightfully declare what constitutes a genuine religious conversion, regardless of its intensity or required time. Whatever it is or however it comes, every genuine Christian change, by definition, must make us more Christlike.

A conversion experience is usually considered to be the first major religious change in our life.

Could it also be erroneous to believe that is the only legitimate conversion we have or need? Perhaps it is necessary to have more than one conversion experience. Pondering this passage raises the possibility that more than one is required. Based primarily upon denominational affiliation, some will vehemently argue that there can be only one. According to them, anyone who claims to have had more than one is seriously mistaken. Others will be as adamant in their support of the opposite view. The possible necessity for more than one religious conversion has strong, extensive and readily available support. Remember Paul had previously been a devout follower of his religious faith. Presumably, he had some kind of conversion and commitment to it. He was haughty and a braggadocio about his pedigree and perfect performance.

His previous conversion experience, whatever it was, did not suffice. Even though he was a devoutly religious man prior to his experience on the Damascus road, he had been seriously mistaken about required religious commitments. A change, another conversion, was required in order to establish a right relationship with God.

Following his initial conversion, whatever and whenever it was, Paul periodically saw the necessity to make adjustments following new insights. It was precisely the same for the disciples of Jesus and it remains the same for us.

Paul's "second" conversion confronts us with our own possible need for another. If more than one is required, perhaps that is another reason we shun the passage! Paul's previous lifestyle may remind us of our own. Like Paul, we may easily become haughty and braggadocios about our religious conversion, commitment and performance. We have often been overly exuberant about our particular brand of religion, with little or no concern for our imitation of Jesus. The line between haughtiness and exuberant witness is not clearly drawn and we may inadvertently and unintentionally cross it. For all of us, there is a frequent need to change all behavior and attitudes that are not conducive to Christ-like living.

 Paulâ€™s need for another conversion calls us to consider that to which we were converted. His experience provides a clear warning to us. We can be just as mistaken about our present religious commitment as he was in his commitment to Judaism.

Even though we think we have exactly what we need, there is a possibility we are mistaken. As a persecutor of Christians, Paul thought he was fulfilling his religious demands. If a learned and religiously dedicated person like Paul can be terribly mistaken, we must exercise extreme caution before issuing any absolutes or practicing haughty behavior in the name of Christian religion. Professing Christians must consciously attempt to be Christ like, to the best of their ability, and repeatedly ask God to convert them again when necessary. Could it be that Judeo-Christian living is a continuous process of tune-ups following an initial conversion? Additional conversions are mandatory if we expect to grow in the faith. None of us can possibly absorb the full dose in one instant application. We learn and change, learn and change… Every devout Christian knows this is personally true. We have serious difficulty arguing for anything else because a large portion of scripture precisely illustrates this process. It was definitely true for ancient Israel.

The disciples of Jesus were unable to instantaneously get it right the first time. Some of them almost never got it right but those who moved in that direction made progress through more than one effort. How can it be different for us?

The more we participate in the faith, the better we understand God's will and purpose. More intricate tuning is desired and required. If every religious change is correctly called a conversion, Christian living is one conversion experience after another. Our required tune- ups may range from minor ones to major overhauls. The conversions that come long after the initial one may also require radical change and may elicit exuberant celebration.

Could it be that we put too much focus on the process of religious conversion experiences and not enough on results? Understanding the basic process is important to us, especially when we facilitate it in others. The important thing is where a person is, not how she/he got there. One's present location is not valued solely by how she/he reached it. Perhaps conversion is similar to a group of people who must climb a mountain from different locations in order to survive. Once they all get to the top, the method by which they got there is not the matter of greatest concern.

No single directive could possibly prescribe the exact number, length and position of every step necessary to get all of them safely to the top. Even though the purpose and result of their journey were almost identical, they had separate needs, individual abilities and all started from a different place. A guide stationed at the peak could call out some helpful hints but each climber must start where he/she was and negotiate his/her personal obstacles as each climbed. Religious conversions are somewhat similar.

Regardless of the particulars in our journey to conversion, it was the action and gift of God to us. In this experience, the end does justify the means. It is an individual thing. Given where we are at its beginning, we may not be able or required to respond like another who is in a very different situation or condition.

The specific steps through which Paul went were useful for him but may be totally useless for others. If we get hung up on the exact sequence or number of necessary steps, if we demand everyone follow our script, the sufficiency of our last conversion may be in serious jeopardy. "Saul" had a script and believed in predetermined steps. An unexpected and unscripted conversion experience changed him into "Paul!"

Could it be that Paul's conversion experience definitely knocked him off his horse? It did! It knocked him off his "high horse." This old southern term precisely describes Paul prior to that experience.

Anyone who acts and insinuates they are superior to others is said to be "on a high horse." Paul was riding high. He was extremely well educated and a recognized scholar on Jewish religion. No one dared question his authority to do whatever he desired to any professing Christian. On his way to Damascus, he was "breathing threats and murder" against anyone who appeared to be a Christian. He felt fully capable of passing religious judgment on any with whom he disagreed and prided himself in his perfect pedigree. Toward Damascus he went, strutting like a peacock and on his "high horse."

Could it be that anyone who rides a "high horse" must be knocked off it if they become or remain truly Christian? Haughtiness, pride and indications of superiority are no part of Christian living. If any professing Christian ever gets on a "high horse," he/she needs to be knocked off because that person is no longer Christian. They must start over, from the ground up. The bright light of God's new revelation blinds them to old ambitions and their immediate future. Previous commitments and activities on which they depended and by which they lived are literally knocked from under them. Recovery and specific redirection take some time. Genuine followers of Christ have no grounds for boasting or feeling superior to others. We are different but not superior. We became what we are through little effort of our own. All we have and are came to us as a gift from God. An infusion of the Christian spirit compels us to be humble before God and our fellowman.

We can no longer be "the cock of the roost" and "the belle of the ball." No one can ride a "high horse" in the Christian parade.
If we ride at all, it must be on a donkey, not on some sleek and prancing thoroughbred that calls attention to itself or its rider.

The story of Paul's conversion provides another major stumbling block for some people. He testified that he regained his sight only after "something like scales fell from his eyes." A literal interpretation of those words provides nothing with which to connect in our personal experience and we have no record of a similar event for anyone other than Paul. Given that, skeptics conclude it was either a "one-time event for a special person" or it did not happen as reported. Either way, it has no value for them and they send it to the religious garbage dump.

A literal interpretation of those words, with absolutely no wiggle room, puts us in a difficult position. Could it be those words are a figure of speech and not meant to be taken literally? If so, that makes Paul's story more applicable and understandable to us. Did he use a physical description for an indescribable religious experience? Could it be the sight he regained was more religious than physical? Paul's inability to see may be in reference to his future and not his actual vision.

His previous religious underpinnings were destroyed, "knocked to the ground," and required him to start over. He was totally unable to ascertain his future. Considering the kind of person he had been, the transforming experiences left him in total disarray, best described as religiously "blind." Even though he was a well-educated religious man entrusted with great Roman authority, he was mentally and spiritually blind because he could not see or anticipate his next move. Few among us comprehend how "blind" Paul must have felt at that moment.

This interpretation finds support in the events that followed. After spending some time with Ananias, "something like scales" fell from Paul's eyes and he regained his sight. How do you adequately describe a transformation from "not seeing" to "seeing?" Cataract surgery removes "something like scales" from one's eye.

A newly discovered solution to a pressing problem removes "something like scales" from the mind's eye and you now see the way to go. If "something like scales" refers to a lack of knowledge and indecision, most of us have been there, religiously and otherwise.

If that is the primary meaning of that phrase, it definitely was not a "one-time event for a special person." It is our story too! Recall your own conversion. None of us knew exactly what we had to do and where we had to go immediately after it? A spectacular conversion experience is often a disturbing experience for us because it makes us unsure of the next step. Most of us knew we were called to be something but we were blind to exactly what the future held for us. There is no more excruciating blindness than this. Eventually our scales of blindness began to fall away as we spoke to our "Ananais," examined the call, talked to other Christians, studied the scriptures, prayed, etc. Perhaps this is a correct description of every conversion experience, not just Paul's.

Something like scales fell from our religious eyes, and perhaps also our minds. In our previous condition, knowingly or unknowingly, we suffered from impaired vision. We may have boasted of what we perceived to be perfect eyesight.

Within our conversion experience, whether initial or subsequent, impediments to proper vision fell away, religiously speaking. Our eyes were opened to some previously unknown or denied truth. After our conversion, we were able to see only after the impediment, something like blinding scales, fell away.

Could it be this passage illustrates how easy it is to have blurred vision in religious matters and not know it? Exuberant commitment, unlimited authority and renowned success are no guarantee a person has perfect vision of God's truth. Consider again the exuberance with which a deeply religious, well-educated and power- possessing Paul pursued and persecuted the Christians, fully convinced he was doing not only what was legal but also precisely what God wanted.

Paul had no monopoly on such behavior. Unless we proceed with great care, professing Christians may suffer from the same malady. Family, denominational and national traditions do not guarantee proper vision. Honest effort and sincere desire are praiseworthy but they do not always insure perfect insight. Just because we see rather well at one time, or under certain circumstance, is no guarantee we always have perfect religious vision.

In spite of all that Paul had going for him, his "vision" was impaired prior to his Christian conversion, and perhaps afterwards. So, it is with us. We will never have perfect religious vision in this life. Even when we see correctly, we do not see completely. God alone is perfect and our religious insights will always be lacking in some respect. Let us remain very humble in sharing what we perceive as ultimate truth because there remains the ever present possibility we are somewhat mistaken and incomplete. If we are mistaken, our humility, openness, sincere trust in God, fervent prayer and a constant effort to be Christ-like will help compensate.

Could it be we often overlook one of the more important points in this passage? Paul began to make sense out of his experience only after he spent extensive time with a previously unknown and devout Christian.

Apparently, Paul initially knew radical and personal change was necessary but he had no idea how to proceed. He was blind in the area of Christian faith and practice. Many years earlier, he sat at Gamaliel's feet and learned the particulars of the Jewish faith. Now he must learn the specifics of the Christian faith. How ironic, the only ones who could instruct him were the very ones he sought to destroy a few days earlier. Like Paul, our vision most often becomes clearer only after spending quality time in the presence of devout Christians. Even though God may deal directly with us and grant personal insight, it is impossible for any individual to properly formulate an independent Christian faith. Too many tried and failed. Paul's conversion was the doorway to his intimate joyful association with other Christians. He learned the essence of faith only from someone who knew it. God did not grant him instant or adequate wisdom in the initial conversion experience.

Here is a valid lesson for any new convert to Christianity, and maybe to some who claim they were converted long ago. A recent genuine conversion does not qualify one to instantly become counselor, guru or pastor of a church. They may be filled with the spirit but they lack appropriate knowledge. Christian living is such a unique, marvelous and different experience we can never instantly decipher its meaning by ourselves. We must maintain intimate and continuous association with others who have ideas of what it means. That association is greatly assisted by colleges and seminaries, commentaries and other good books.

Some professing Christians believe that one instantaneous and cataclysmic conversion experience provides everything needed to be and remain fully Christian. They think it sufficiently equips them to properly fulfill any task to which they feel called. Believing they have been gloriously converted, they turn loose of a plow, quit their day job, walk out of the kitchen, etc. and begin to preach without learning from others what it is all about. We applaud their commitment but question their response. They may proudly boast they have and need no formal education and may even condemn those who do.

 We must ask, "Are they reasonably equipped for Christian ministry?" Paul didn't preach until he spent considerable time with those who truly knew Jesus. Even though well educated, he needed additional and proper training before he could fulfill his calling. After he became a proclaimer of the gospel, he maintained close association with and learned from other Christians. Could it be any different for us?

Could it be Paul associated with other Christians not only to better understand his initial conversion but also to assist with necessary tune-ups, if and when needed? Here is another lesson for all professing Christians. It is almost impossible to maintain faithful Christian living while isolated from other genuine Christians. We are accountable to and for others. A need for community lies at the core of our existence as individuals and Christians. That is how God made us. Therefore, all those flimsy, instant and cute excuses for failure to participate in any organized religious group fall flat on their face.

Some may reflect a speck of truth but they are always incomplete and insufficient. Lack of participation does not necessarily keep one from being a relatively good person but it greatly diminishes the possibility of being a good and growing Christian.

Could it be this passage declares the ever-present possibility for conversion, regardless of how wicked someone may appear? From the early Christians' perspective, there was no one more evil than Paul. From their perspective, his conversion was desirable. No records indicate they did anything to encourage or hasten his demise. We have no way of knowing but perhaps they prayed for and about him. If God can effect the conversion of a powerful, evil and misinformed man like Paul, apparently no one is beyond that possibility.

Even though there are some people in our day who are correctly called evil and in need of conversion, we cannot perfectly identify them. From where we stand and from our human point of view, our Christian response is to only surmise. We must not judge but we may exercise our rights as a humble fruit inspector. This passage of scripture provides no justification, authority or ability to publicly declare who needs a conversion or who had one.

Could it be this passage declares a conversion may come at any time, in any place and under unusual conditions? Paul was not in an eleven o'clock worship service on a Sunday morning, in a revival meeting or at a youth camp. There was no well-known evangelist tearfully begging him to come kneel at the altar as the congregation sang eighteen verses of "Just As I Am." There were no threats of eternal damnation to the fiery pits of hell for dastardly deeds done against the servants of God.

Right there on the highly traveled, dusty, country road, with a bunch of unsavory characters and without religious signs or symbols or script, it happened! That so called unusual spot for a conversion may not be as unusual as we first thought. Conversions came to people in strange and unexpected places because they met God there.

Read the Bible! If professing Christians would give up their selfish desire to protect personal and denominational turf, more modern-day conversions would take place far beyond the walls of the church building.

When Christians live and act as they ought, conversions occur in drug and alcohol rehab centers, homeless shelters, crisis centers, work places, recreational facilities, snack bars, etc. Time and time again, that is where the seed is planted and the change is initiated, for good or evil. When religious leaders and participants are more concerned with adding another number to their denomination than in facilitating genuine Christian living, far fewer conversions will come in unusual places, as well as in usual ones.

Could it be this passage forcefully reminds us that religious conversions are God's business? Perhaps that is why Paul's conversion occurred when and where it did. Otherwise, someone would have wanted credit for such an accomplishment. Genuine Christians do not keep an account of how many they "saved." They don't need to because they didn't "save" anyone. Even if they did, counting would indicate selfish concerns. "Saving people" is God's business. Assuming full credit for another person's conversion is idolatry. None of us are ever more than partially instrumental in God's process for religious conversion of another person. Countless other Christians participated in the collective witness that ultimately enabled God to effect a conversion.

Our primary responsibility is to witness constantly about him who makes all things new. We have no need or right to notch our personal prayer shawl or put another star on our Bible when someone to whom we witnessed experiences a conversion. Could it be that this passage clearly indicates the delayed effectiveness of witnessing? Paul was eventually converted primarily because of previous Christian witness and lifestyle? None of those witnesses were with him on the road to Damascus. Those to whom he brought death and misery left an indelible imprint on his life by the way they lived, suffered and died. They were the primary instruments through which God broke into Paul's life.

Could it be that God always works like that? If he does, the responsibility of all genuine Christians is clear. If we want God to work in another person's life, regardless of how wicked we may think they are, let us imitate as best we can the action of Christ. If our witness enables a conversion of another, praise God for it. If no religious conversion comes to them, we have done all we could for their good and we have done what we should. To do otherwise does harm to them and us.

Paul's conversion was significant to him, just as our conversion was/is significant to us. Following a meticulous examination of his
story, we realize it is our story too. It is not a "one-time special event for a special person" but it is the story of every person who experienced a genuine religious conversion. Its broader application provides applicable insights for all who seek to become and remain genuinely Christian. Apparently, those who disregard it and declare it irrelevant do so for one of two reasons. Either they are fearful of what it demands of them or they are grossly misinformed.

CHAPTER EIGHT
Disturbing Directives
1 Thessalonians 5:14-22

14: And we exhort you, brethren, admonish the idlers, encourage the fainthearted, help the weak, be patient with them all.

15: See that none of you repays evil for evil, but always seek to do good to one another and to all.

16: Rejoice always,

17: pray constantly,

18: give thanks in all circumstances; for this is the will of God in Christ Jesus for you.

19: Do not quench the Spirit,

20: do not despise prophesying,

21: but test everything; hold fast what is good,

22: abstain from every form of evil.

Paul's expressed requirements for Christian living are often considered impractical and impossible. Having been identified as one or the other, if not both, this passage joins the list of irrelevant and ridiculous scriptures relegated to the garbage heap.

The argument for irrelevancy has some support. Paul probably wrote these words as ethical and religious requirements for those living in "the last days." If we properly interpret what he wrote, he and the Christian community eagerly expected the immediate return of Christ and the end of time.

If Christ was returning soon, these requirements had a profound urgency for all Christians in their final preparation for the next life. Anyone expecting to be "Taken up with Christ" at his return must keep these requirements. Paul admonished Christians to live as he directed during the short period of time remaining.

Christ did not return as Paul and the early Christians anticipated. If Paul gave these directives to those people living in that time and under those conditions, how relevant are they today? Our world and expectations radically differ from theirs. Therefore, do we totally disregard the words, as some argue, or do we examine them from a new perspective?

Some people say Paul's directives should be disregarded because they demand something absolutely impossible, whether then or now. If they demand the impossible, that makes them absurd and irrelevant. Their argument has a point, but it is not a valid point. Could it be they argue primarily because they either seek to avoid binding requirements or have grossly misunderstood them? Perhaps we have encountered another passage we may retrieve from the trash heap with a new interpretation.

Could it be Paul meant precisely what he said, whether speaking to early Christians or to us? If we conveniently convince ourselves that Paul spoke only to those of his day, we completely escape any responsibility to live by his directives. If the directives are also addressed to us, we must seriously ponder their possible meaning or else run the risk of putting our religious life in serious jeopardy. If we disregard these directives, for whatever reason we may manufacture, our religious life is far less demanding. If we accept their validity, they infringe upon our carefree living.

Paul's words in this passage are properly understood only when placed in the context of his overall teachings. They were never meant to be isolated and interpreted apart from his total thoughts. If these simple phrases are interpreted in isolation, erroneous conclusions are easily and inevitably reached. Vastly different conclusions come when interpreted within the context of his total theology and teachings.

No one in our day completely understands the theology of Paul. Some say he did not understand it either! Noted scholars have written volumes attempting to explain and interpret the meaning of his many words. This is not the place to relate or review his theology but we must remember it affected all he said and did.

Much of what he said in this passage is applicable to us. Verses sixteen, seventeen and eighteen are most troublesome for many professing Christians. Two of Paul's three directives, "Rejoice always" (v.16) and "Give thanks in all circumstances" (v. 18) will be addressed in this chapter. The third directive, for continuous prayer (v. 17), deserves separate treatment and is the subject of the following chapter. Verse sixteen admonishes us to rejoice always. How could Paul expect the early Christians to do that? They lived under very difficult circumstances and were often unpopular, ridiculed and persecuted. At certain times and in certain places, anyone who publicly professed adherence to the Christian persuasion made themselves candidates for prison or death. Daily existence was always dangerous and doubtful. How can anyone rejoice under those circumstances?

Let us take this matter a step further and make it personal. Given our present circumstances, how can anyone rejoice constantly? No person is completely free from sorrow, pain and disappointment. There are some parts of the world where it may not be good for your health to publicly profess Christian commitments. Even in places where it is not a life threatening event, it may jeopardize employment, professional practice, and social standing. The trend in America is to take religious references and particular religious practices from public view. Prayer at public gatherings, prominent display of Christian symbols or words, and public acknowledgment of God's sovereignty are frowned upon, if not illegal. How can modern Christians rejoice constantly?

If one rejoices only after daily existence is easy, safe and perfectly satisfying, all Christians had and have little over which to rejoice. Paul knew that and never asked or expected his followers to accept or encourage adverse circumstances as the primary basis for rejoicing.

Something far more important is the foundation of genuine joy. He encouraged all Christians to rejoice not because of our physical conditions but in spite of them. What God had done, is doing and will do for and in us is more important than anything else. God is greater than anything our situation can produce, whether good or ill.

Regardless of the other circumstances, God's activity and presence among us provide adequate grounds for rejoicing. We have something greater than human comfort that enables us to rejoice in the midst of human misery, not because of it! A simple preposition makes a major difference. Paul's theology and religious teachings affirmed the power and presence of God who would eventually give a just reward to all who remain faithfully committed to him. When that firm belief undergirds all Christians, when they fully recognize that, they are able to rejoice in the face of adversity, not because of it.

Well-meaning advocates of Christian beliefs have misinterpreted Paul's primary point and believe Christians are to rejoice because they have troubles. For some, serious adversity is interpreted as a special blessing from God and proof that a person is genuinely Christian. The point is illustrated by the person who said, "Thank God, my house burned down." For those who accept that absurd theology, having problems apparently becomes the criteria for judging the amount of their faith and commitment. Adversity seems to be welcomed so they may make a strong witness.

The early Christians demonstrated a firm commitment when they endured painful death rather than deny their faith. Practicing their faith first got them in trouble and their faith enabled them to fearlessly meet death. It was not a persecuted life or a horrible death that gave them their faith. They did not rejoice because they were persecuted. They rejoiced in spite of the persecution. They would have rejoiced without persecution!

Throughout history, Christians experienced trouble of some sort. We must admit, under certain circumstances and situations, Christian commitments may cause additional problems in this life.

Given the conditions under which we live, the correlation of problems to commitments has a minute measure of truth but that does not mean we should rejoice when trouble comes. Troubles are no proof or proper measurement of Christian commitments. Those who misinterpret Paul's request and welcome pain and trouble produce additional problems for all of us.

Paul never said there is no Christian life if there is no adversity. That interpretation makes God a monster who delights in our misery, one who makes us miserable so that we will worship him. It also suggests a Christian's life will always be painful and the amount of adversity confronted is synonymous with the degree of Christian commitment. Jesus certainly taught otherwise.

Could it be that Paul's reason to rejoice focuses on the purpose and presence of God, not on the presence or absence of human discomfort? God's abiding presence and purpose are the primary sources of our genuine joy, not persistent persecution and pain.

Paul's approach does not deny the desire or need for human comfort in this life. He does not suggest physical comfort is unholy or harmful. For him, there is something far more important for Christians. We continually rejoice over having what is mosti mportant, even when physical life is painful and uncertain. Under no condition do we purposely invite adversity, rejoice when it comes or use it to measure commitment.

Paul provides another specific directive in verse eighteen when he says "Give thanks in all circumstances." Taken out of context or misinterpreted, this directive also poses problems for many. This directive is basically the same as the first one discussed above, with "give thanks" substituted for "rejoice always." Having already closely examined his first request, this one needs little additional attention. Most comments made about the first are helpful in understanding this directive and make it less problematic.

Once again, a little preposition makes a large difference. Paul requested Christians to give thanks "in" and not "for" all circumstances. Another key word is "thanks," not "circumstances."
Paul was convinced all Christians are thankful to God for what he has done and is doing in and for them. God is always in ultimate control, not the circumstances. Recognition of that fact gives every Christian something for which to be thankful at all times and in all situations.

Once again, he emphasizes God's action and not human comfort. Paul was not thankful for the circumstances that produced pain and death for the early Christians. He no doubt vehemently despised it but that did not cause him to accuse God of purposefully inflicting misery on people. If Paul thanked God for the painful circumstances, God would be the provider of the misery. A God who goes around purposely inflicting pain on people in order to provide something for which they can be thankful is less than a loving God. Apparently, some modern-day professing Christians do not understand for what we are to be thankful. When they thank God for burning down their house, causing a car wreck, losing their job, etc., their concept of God is questionable, they blame God for something he didn't necessarily do and they have seriously misunderstood what Paul asked of us.

In 1 Thessalonians 5:16&18, Paul makes two difficult requests of Christians. Rightfully understood, they are not impractical or impossible. Under no condition should we relegate those requirements for the early Christians to the religious garbage dump. They are not special requirements in a special time for a special group. They are for anyone who seeks to be genuinely Christian. His ardent requests had little to do with his belief that the end of time was near. They are not unnecessary requirements dreamed up by an eccentric evangelist. The requirements are not a matter of choice for

Christians, in Paul's day or today. They reflect a profound understanding of what it means to live a Christian life. They are the automatic overflow from anyone who seeks to maintain the proper relationship with God. We do ourselves a disservice if we delete, dilute or disregard these admonitions.

CHAPTER NINE
IS THAT POSSIBLE?
I Thessalonians 5:17

17: Pray constantly

If the two directives discussed in the previous chapter are difficult to follow, what about the third one? Paul presents another seemingly impossible request in verse seventeen, instructing us to "Pray constantly" or "without ceasing. "(NRSV) Most of us believe it is impossible to do that. If we accept his admonition without explanation or interpretation, all of us have failed to fulfill it. Given our human condition and nature, we have little hope of ever accomplishing it. If it is physically impossible to accomplish, why did Paul request it and why bother with it?

Paul either went too far or most of us have much more to learn about prayer. Those who believe he went too far use that as justification to trash the passage. Others go to great lengths to justify its validity exactly as it stands. Many scholars, preachers and Sunday school teachers accept the validity of his request, simply because it is in the Bible. They offer diverse and exotic explanations to soften it and explain why he really didn't mean what he actually said. Many of us ponder Paul's instructions to pray without ceasing and need help to either fulfill it or to better understand it.

Could it be that Paul did not go too far but rather we have not gone far enough? Our confusion or clarification is contained in our definition of prayer? Paul did not give us a precise definition. No one can give a complete, all encompassing and absolute definition acceptable and meaningful to everyone. Most of us have some understanding of prayer, even if inadequate and incomplete. Our understanding and practice of prayer was first absorbed during our formative years from others with whom we associated. We mostl ikely absorbed it without an invitation, question, comment, or alteration. If our teacher's approach was positive and appropriate,
ours is similar.

If their understanding was inaccurate and incomplete, ours has a strong tendency to be the same. If their prayers had very limited dimension or precise particulars, so do ours.

Before we can properly respond to Paul's request, we must decide precisely what he asked us to do. If we were to poll every Christian congregation, a majority would describe prayer primarily as something we do. It often begins and ends there, regardless of the circuitous route and many words used to express one's understanding of it. Most of our teaching and examples from parents or religious leaders led us to that assumption. The major portion of our conversations pertaining to prayer contains words that indicate action, or doing something. We attempt to "do" prayer. Here is the primary problem with following Paul's directive because it is difficult,i f not impossible, to constantly "do something." Therefore, it seems we must either disregard Paul's directive or pursue another understanding of prayer.

Many believe prayer is an individual or collective activity through which and in which we seek to influence God's action. It is our deliberate action designed to get God's response. If prayer is doing something designed to influence God's response, it is wise to pray often and it is necessary when in deep difficulty. Most often, such prayer is designed and dedicated to make God aware of our or another's needs but not designed to make us more aware of God's demands and desires. In many instances, what we commonly call prayer is little more than an attempt to bargain with God, especially when we are in a serious situation created primarily by our own stupidity and for which we see no human solution. We believe it is permissible to promise God something if he will give us what we want, get us out of a jam, or suspend divine and human laws for just this one time.

When prayer is basically understood as something we do, praying involves little use of our mind and the extensive use of words. We utter words in an attempt to convey our thoughts and desires to God. Having repeatedly uttered the same words in the same way while asking for the same thing, we may become so automatic in what we say and do that we fail to really think about it.

We "spin our prayer wheel" containing previously prepared and prepackaged prayers. It is as if we read the words off the back of our eyelids. We appear to be on auto pilot or stuck in a rut. We thoughtlessly recite the words prescribed by others or memorized on our own. If we carefully listen to our prayers, and the prayers of others, we may be surprised how often words reflect our failure to think about what we say and are exact replicas of previous prayers. Thoughtless prayer reflects poor theology that includes ideas we would not otherwise accept, like praying for God to "be with" someone as if he is not already there.

Many of us were taught, and we now automatically assume, prayers must be offered according to a prescribed format or they are ineffective. Every head must be bowed, every eye closed, on our knees, hands folded in a prescribed manner, one or both hands held high overhead, offered in a specific place and at a certain time, etc. Some people say a genuine prayer must always end with the words
"In the name of Jesus. Amen." If that is true, Jewish people of all ages have been and are now unable to pray!

Prayer interpreted from the perspective of "doing something" emphasizes asking God to do something for us, either directly or indirectly. Except on very rare occasions, it contains no new offer of our praise or assistance to God, no expressed willingness to be presently obedient to his will and no volunteer statement for some hazardous duty. It expresses no willingness to be damned for the glory of God!
Too frequently, our prayers resemble the renewal of a standing order to a catalogue department where we simply check the blocks that delineate our demands, followed by announcing our expectations for immediate delivery. If the items are unavailable, we expect something nearest our stated choice, but better and at the same price.

The effectiveness of this kind of prayer is most often measured by external signs. If the project was successfully completed, the journey safely ended, the rains came or quit, the sick recovered, the bill paid, etc., the prayers were considered genuine, effective and answered.

If some of these prayers were not answered as expected, the one who prayed, or another, easily concluded something must have been wrong with what they did. Certain questions immediately follow. Did the prayer contain correct words, format, time, place, position of body parts, etc.? In most cases, either the one who prayed or a well- meaning and a self-appointed authority identifies the flaw that prevented the prayer's effectiveness. The person carefully and deliberately repeats the prescribed process, at least for a few times.

If prayer primarily refers to something we do, that understanding is fraught with danger. It is impossible to pray constantly. It allows us to determine what constitutes a valid prayer, not God. If prayer is communication, not much communication takes place because God often remains silent. It places too much emphasis on our effort. It also disregards human nature and the nature of God. It prevents prayer from being joyful, meaningful and genuine Christian worship.

One who believes they have sincerely "done" proper prayers but repeatedly received no satisfactory answer begins to question the value of prayer and what they were taught about it. Their repeated prayers that have no desired results may soon cause them to doubt the existence of God, God's concern for them and their worth to him. How long will they even try to pray?

Could it be that what we commonly call prayer may not be prayer at all? Even though it is necessary to "do" something when we pray, prayer must be more than "doing" or it isn't genuine prayer. At best, prayer that focuses on "doing" is an ill-advised and legalistic effort to be Christian. At its worst, it is an attempt to manipulate God for human pleasure, and that is unchristian. When we recognize that such an approach to prayer defames God and denigrates us, we realize the immediate necessity for a different approach.

Prayer is grounded in our theology, in what we believe about God. Fundamental beliefs largely determine our behavior. If our theology is inappropriate, our approach to prayer will be inappropriate.

If our theology is appropriate, our prayers will be appropriate in form and fervor. Intellectually, we readily admit genuine prayer is not between equals nor is it from the greater to the lesser. We verbally affirm the sovereignty of God in every area of life but often pray as if we own him, are equal to him or can bargain with him.

If we "pray" like that, something is seriously amiss in our theology and prayer.

A different definition and understanding of prayer help dissolve our dilemma. Genuine prayer focuses first on "being," and then on "doing." It is best defined or described primarily as something we are, something that bubbles up from within and flows from the depth of our being. It comes from the core of our being that is in a right relationship with God. It can never be generated solely by what we do. What we do in genuine prayer is and must always be secondary to what we are.

This understanding of prayer involves our heart or soul. From the Judeo-Christian perspective, the only foundation for genuine prayer is a particular relationship between God and us. We commonly describe this relationship as having our heart right with God. In the most literal sense, only those who are in the proper relationship with God can truly pray. Anyone out of that proper relationship may speak prescribed words, put them in a designated order and properly position themselves but they have not truly prayed. Mental gymnastics performed according to prescribed rules is not prayer but only an attempt to perform religious magic. From this perspective, those who do not consciously recognize God's sovereignty are unable to genuinely pray, no matter what they do.

Genuine prayer comes from being in a right relationship with God. That is true for the first feeble prayer of a repentant sinner and the unspoken prayer of a seasoned saint. By definition, prayer can never be flippant, perfunctory, self-centered, demanding, deceitful, an attempt to bargain, bound by certain words, measured by a fixed format, or even limited to words.

Genuine prayer reflects and is the result of a proper relationship with God at the core of our being. We will not demonstrate the sovereignty of God if he is not sovereign over us. We cannot act humbly if we are basically haughty. We cannot fake joyful servant- hood if we are not joyful and willing servants. We cannot give thanks if thankfulness does not abide in us.

We are unable to offer praise if we aren't deeply appreciative of what God has done and is doing for us. We cannot commit ourselves to his service if we seek to be served by him. We cannot successfully pretend to be what we aren't. Behavior indicates being. We must possess and be possessed by a Christ-like nature, spirit, attitude and likeness in order to pray effectively.

A proper relationship with God also demands extensive use of our mind. Emotional religious expressions are quite acceptable and possibly encouraged but senseless behavior under the guise of worship is an abomination. If we consciously desire a right relationship with God, we must frequently and fervently contemplate what that means and how to maintain it. A conversion experience does not provide all the answers. God gave us a mind and expects mental activity from us in order to fulfill our purpose for being. God made us for his purpose. He is the loving master and we are his servants. We were created as his helpers, not his equal. If we ever forget or momentarily disregard these facts, we change who we are in the core of our being and that changes our behavior. A deliberate and diligent use of our mind is necessary in order to have any chance of imitating God's being and behavior in our "being" and "doing."

Genuine prayer mentally recognizes God's sovereignty and involves a mental response to him for who he is and for what he has already done for us. Cessation of mental activity leads to selfishness. Even though concerns for "self" are very important, we have renounced our proper relationship with God if they dominate our attempt to pray, no matter how well we have camouflaged our selfishness. It is most helpful to open every conscious prayer with an honest acknowledgment of who God is and who we are.

That acknowledgment keeps us mentally alert, helps us humbly enter the master's presence, reminds us we are the guests who may enter only because the master permits and prescribes how we must act therein. Otherwise, it is so easy to assume we are praying when we are not.

A right relationship with God involves a right relationship with all God's creation. Genuine prayer must always reflect our place in the created order and our treatment of all God created. No person can truly pray who deliberately destroys and woefully wastes anything in God's creation. Such behavior disregards, if it does not deny, the sovereignty of God.

Our relationship with God affects our relationship with his people. If we are out of the proper relationship with God's people, we are also out of relationship with him and therefore cannot really pray.

Recall the New Testament story in Matt. 5:23-24 that clearly states we cannot truly worship until we are first reconciled with our brother. In that situation, our "being" is out of a proper relationship not only with our brother but also with God.

A proper relationship with God requires us, to the best of our ability, to treat ourselves as God treats us. Improper thoughts about "self" prevent the proper relationship with God and pervert genuine pray. Christian living is a constant effort to balance thoughts about ourselves so that we never attempt to be above the human level and never move below it. Improper thoughts pertaining to ourselves are expressed in two opposite directions. On one hand, we tend to think more highly of "self" than we ought and then act accordingly. On the other hand, we may consider ourselves worthless or terribly flawed and act accordingly. The improper evaluation of self is an ever present danger against which we fight, especially if God has abundantly blessed us, if our life is filled with trouble or if we lack self-esteem.

Biblical writers speak of the danger in thinking more highly of ourselves than we ought but address the opposite only by inference. The number of victims who presently suffer from low self-esteem is alarming and increases daily. If the malady was common in biblical times, the subject appears to have been basically ignored. It debilitates life to a degree not recognized by the average person. Low self-esteem disrupts one's personal/religious life and is a definite detraction to genuine prayer.

Could it be that the Disciples knew what we do not know? A well-known New Testament story records Jesus' attempt to teach them how to pray (Matt. 6:5-15). Could it be they were not seeking exact verbiage, a prescribed format or the proper body positions for doing something that could be correctly called prayer? Were they simply asking Jesus to teach them how to be in his likeness and nature? Did they long to be like him, to be in and live in a proper relationship with God? Was their request "Help us get there?" Perhaps they did not ask Jesus to "Teach us proper words, positions and format."

Could it be that the prayer Jesus provided is properly offered only by those who are in a positive relationship with God? The opening and closing portions of Jesus' prayer defines the necessary relationship. The requests in the middle of the prayer hinge upon an existing proper relationship.

A perfect repetition of the verbiage without a proper relationship to God and others is less than genuine prayer. Describing prayer from the perspective of "being" more than "doing" makes a radical difference at many points. It enables us to fulfill the request of Paul who invited us to pray constantly. It enables us to meet the requirement without mental gymnastics or playing word games in order to justify scripture. It agrees with fundamental theology and practical sense. It honestly affirms that we are able to continually be in the spirit of prayer but we are unable to constantly do a prescribed act.

This approach necessitates changes in the way we think and talk about prayer. It is not primarily doing something but it is being Christ-like. It is not just audible words but it is primarily an inner spirit and attitude. It is now most appropriate for the leader in a worship service to announce prayer time with "Let us be in prayer" instead of "Let us pray." The first announcement reflects the true nature of genuine prayer but the second sounds as if we are to "do" prayer. Most of us will need practice before we learn to talk first about prayer as something we are and then as something we do.

Genuine prayer eventually requires us to "do" something, but the doing must always come from our being. Having humble hearts filled with awe and gratitude, we pour forth praise, petitions, confessions, etc. as a conscious act of worship on the pathway to joyful and obedient service. What we periodically do in genuine prayer has meaning only because it comes from what we are, from the right spirit within us. We have a complete prayer life only if we periodically do something but the doing and the being must be kept in the proper order. That is what it means to be Christian. This new approach to prayer provides no external criteria by which to judge its validity or determine why it was "unanswered."

Perhaps we speak of answered and unanswered prayer only when prayer is considered something we do. Could it be that genuine prayer has no need or concern for exact and measurable answers? A demand for recognizable answers possibly means we are not only selfish but also praying improperly and, according to our new understanding of prayer, that may not be real prayer after all.

Genuine prayer reflects a complete confidence in God, assured he will always grant our humble and unselfish requests according to his will and not according to our wants. If we are in genuine prayer, we need no specific response at a specified time, even though it would be welcomed. If there is a problem here, it is with us and not with God. Could it be we are sometimes deep in prayer without uttering a word? A few passages of scripture suggest that possibility.

We desire a continuous relationship with God and seek to avoid moving in and out of it, as difficult as that may be. Heart, soul and mind are open and receptive to God's eternal truth.

We eagerly look and reverently listen for God's presence in the common occurrences of everyday life.
Our silent and sure recognition, deep appreciation and genuine enjoyment of the mysteries and wonders of God's spectacular creation may indeed be genuine parts of true prayer. Every unpremeditated act of Christian love illustrates our relationship with God and encompasses true prayer.

Could we genuinely pray without knowing it? The previous paragraph alludes to that possibility. Given our new understanding of prayer, it seems our spirit, the core of our being, can be in unconscious communion with God's spirit. If so, that is prayer at its deepest possible level, reached only after we are saturated with the spirit of God, only after obedience, awe, praise, thanksgiving, etc. guide our every action. Given our nature, this saturation experiencei s the goal toward which we strive and the direction of our travel. On rare occasions and under unique circumstances, we may reach the goal, but most often we have a distance to go. Could it be that unconscious prayer also occurs at a vastly different level? Is the unconscious and conscious cry for meaning and purpose in life also genuine prayer?

Is the created image and spirit of God dwelling in us crying for recognition and response? Was this the first prayer prayed by every one of us, even though it was unconsciously prayed and possibly addressed to an unknown God?

Could it be the one true prayer hidden in the heart of all who have not consciously responded to God?It comes from who we are as a part of God's creation. Our basic spirit cries out to God's spirit, but we may not know what it is or how to respond. Many of us would not call that prayer but perhaps it is precisely that.

Could it be that prayer is the "book ends" of our life as God intended it? Human nature has the innate and unconscious plea for meaning. In unconscious prayer, our very being cries out for meaning. As life continues, some of us fortunately find the proper relationship with God and endeavor to embody his image and imitate his action. When that becomes ingrained in us and we are best described as being consciously and unconsciously in tune with God, we participate in the highest form of prayer. We become what God created us to be and do. Our life's journey led us from the basic unconscious prayer, through conscious prayer and finally back to the highest form of unconscious prayer. The first stage is chaos, the second is commitment and the last is communion. The journey from the first stage to the last is not guaranteed, automatic or easy but it is our developmental route designed by God? This book-end theory about unconscious prayer may sound strange but is appears to be excellent theology. Can we fulfill Paul's request to pray without ceasing? The answer is found in our definition and understanding of prayer. If we understand prayer as primarily something we do according to specific directives, we can never "pray constantly," no matter how hard we try. Our human limitations restrain us. If we understand prayer as a reflection and expression of a right relationship with God, we are at least able to be in the spirit of and desire for prayer at all times. A proper relationship with God enables us to maintain a prayerful spirit. That relationship is the underlying thrust and directive for everything we do. Maintaining that constant relationship is the goal of every Christian and the ideal lifestyle to which Paul called us.

CHAPTER TEN
EASTER: EVENT or EXPERIENCE?
John 20:1-18

1: Now on the first day of the week Mary Mag'dalene came to the tomb early, while it was still dark, and saw that the stone had been taken away from the tomb.

2: So she ran, and went to Simon Peter and the other disciple, the one whom Jesus loved, and said to them, "They have taken the Lord out of the tomb, and we do not know where they have laid him."

3: Peter then came out with the other disciple, and they went toward the tomb.

4: They both ran, but the other disciple outran Peter and reached the tomb first;

5: and stooping to look in, he saw the linen cloths lying there, but he did not go in.

6: Then Simon Peter came, following him, and went into the tomb; he saw the linen cloths lying,

7: and the napkin, which had been on his head, not lying with the linen cloths but rolled up in a place by itself.

8: Then the other disciple, who reached the tomb first, also went in, and he saw and believed;

9: for as yet they did not know the scripture, that he must rise from the dead.

10: Then the disciples went back to their homes.
11: But Mary stood weeping outside the tomb, and as she wept, she stooped to look into the tomb;

12: and she saw two angels in white, sitting where the body of Jesus had lain, one at the head and one at the feet.

13: They said to her, "Woman, why are you weeping?" She said to them, "Because they have taken away my Lord, and I do not know where they have laid him."

14: Saying this, she turned around and saw Jesus standing, but she did not know that it was Jesus.

15: Jesus said to her, "Woman, why are you weeping? Whom do you seek?" Supposing him to be the gardener, she said to him, "Sir, if you have carried him away, tell me where you have laid him, and I will take him away."

16: Jesus said to her, "Mary." She turned and said to him in Hebrew, "Rab-bo'ni!" (which means Teacher).

17: Jesus said to her, "Do not hold me, for I have not yet ascended to the Father; but go to my brethren and say to them, I am ascending to my Father and your Father, to my God and your God."

18: Mary Mag'dalene went and said to the disciples, "I have seen the Lord"; and she told them that he had said these things to her.

Can it be that Easter is always either an event or an experience for everyone? There is a radical difference between the two. In fact, that difference largely separates genuine Christians from those who are classified as something else. That difference largely determines whether we take seriously the biblical reports of Easter or relegate them to the religious garbage dump.

Overly simple definitions may help us separate an experience from an event. An event is something that happens outside and beyond us. We stand outside and away from it. We are not consciously involved in an event and are most often unaware of it when it happens It is something about which we may or may not have later heard or seen evidence.

Some events indirectly and unknowingly affect us even when we are unaware of them. Having heard, read or seen evidence of an event, we may ignore it, deny it, disbelieve it, accept it, etc. Conversely, we stand in the midst of an experience or perhaps it is in the midst of us! It is a part of us. An experience encompasses an event in which we are involved. Our experience may be only an event for another person, if they become aware of it. One experience may not have the same intensity as another. A lost comb has far less intensity than a lost fortune but each is an experience for the one to whom it happened. An experience shared by more than one person may not equally affect everyone to whom it came. Our hearing about an event, or discovering evidence of it, is an experience of hearing or discovery, not an experience of the event about which we heard or have evidence. We cannot deny, disbelieve or disregard an experience without possible grave danger. Our emotions are unavoidably affected, to some degree, by an experience whereas they may or may not be noticeably affected in the aftermath of an event. No event will ever make the same impact as an experience.

The stories of Easter repeatedly illustrate the vast differences between an event and an experience. In John's Gospel, Mary Magdalene had an experience at the empty tomb but her account of it was a reported event to the disciples. It was up to them to decide what to do about the report. The disciples' hearing and response to her report were experiences for them. Each of the four New Testament Gospels provides a few different details about Easter's events. Taken individually or collectively, they provide no complete account of the events of Easter or of the disciples' experiences related to them. Regardless of their differences, each Gospel boldly affirms the mystery of the Resurrection. Those events were reported as experiences for someone or for several people.

John's gospel reports that Mary Magdalene went alone to the tomb before daybreak on what we now call "Sunday morning." It gives no reason for her visit or why she went at that specific time. Each reader must make his/her own assumption. It seems wise to surmise she was at least going to show her respect and devotion to Jesus.

Could it have been something more significant that compelled her to go, either alone or in the company of others? If she was the woman who had experienced a radical religious transformation by Jesus, we can understand why she went to the tomb. If she had been one of his ardent supporters, as it seems she was, then it was only natural that she wished to visit his burial site. If there were unfinished religious rituals to be accomplished, we can easily
understand her haste to get to the tomb. If she was Jesus' wife, as some have suggested, she had further reason to hasten her visit.

Could it be that the "Mary' who went alone to the tomb was none other than the mother of Jesus? That possibility is not as radical as we may first think. Since these stories were originally transmitted orally and were put into written form many years after the event, it is highly possible that someone easily misidentified the "Mary" in the story. If so, it was not intentional but illustrates one of the simple things that can easily happen when events are verbally reported long afterwards by those who did not experience them. When two or more people with the same name participate in an event, it becomes difficult for others who later tell the story to keep them in their proper place. Who would be more likely to immediately visit the tomb than his mother? It is ludicrous for us to assume that Jesus' mother would not
be among the first to visit the tomb. We have various other reported details that do not exactly agree. If the Mary at the tomb in this story was actually the mother of Jesus, we can easily understand why his grief stricken mother was there.

Upon reaching the tomb, Mary was deeply surprised to find something or someone had removed the huge stone from the tomb's entrance. According to John's report, without any delay or further examination of the tomb, she hastily returned to the location of two disciples. One of those disciples was Peter and the other is identified only as "the one whom Jesus loved." How strange! We normally assume Jesus loved each and every disciple. Why did John make such a statement? There must be some plausible explanation for this most unusual identification. Scholars have suggested that "the other disciple" was none other than the author of this story.

If so, he had his own reasons to remain anonymous. Otherwise, we have no plausible explanation for the strange verbiage. Having heard Mary's report that "They have taken the Lord out of the tomb and we do not know where they have laid him," the two disciples experienced a foot-race to the tomb.

Mary's use of the word "we" confuses the issue and we wonder if she was accompanied by others, if she consulted with others prior to reaching the two disciples, if she just used the plural word for her own reason, or if this may be a later interpretation designed to bring this report into harmony with others. It also seems rather odd that Mary made that bold announcement if she only saw the stone removed and did not first check to see if the body was there.

According to John's report, impetuous Peter once again charged ahead without questions or consultation. Could it be that this time he had a good reason? We aren't sure what he believed about the stories Jesus reportedly told regarding "Resurrection." If Peter had any recollection of them and any hope of their truthfulness, there is no wonder he raced to the tomb. Additionally, the burning agony of his recent denial would not go away. Had he verbally and repeatedly flogged himself for having been unfaithful? Had he longed for another chance to prove his loyalty and commitment to the cause? Had he frequently recalled and repeated the words of Jesus, hoping to find some meaning to the crucifixion experience? While racing breathlessly to the tomb, he may have asked over and over, "Could Jesus possibly be yet alive?" Had he also rehearsed in his mind what he would say to Jesus, if he only had the chance? Mary's exuberant announcement may have rekindled hope that all was not lost and that Jesus was alive. How could Peter keep from running?

Could it be that Peter's quick departure toward the tomb was prompted by something less? If Mary's reported event was little more than that to him, just a reported event, then perhaps he could find Jesus' body and properly care for it. He owed that much to Jesus and to Mary, especially if she was the mother or wife of Jesus.

If he could recover the misplaced body and properly dispose of it, that might help ease his and her inner pain. We wonder if there were some religious requirements for proper disposition of the deceased and if Peter was only seeking to fulfill those requirements. We have no answers.

For whatever reason, Peter and the unnamed disciple reportedly raced to the tomb. Peter lost the race but was the first of the two to enter it. Even though the other disciple was the last to enter, he was the first to recognize the significance of what they saw. The wrappings that had bound Jesus were positioned in such a way that no person could have removed the wrappings from the body of Jesus and replaced them as they lay.

The condition and position of the wrappings bore witness to the fact that something extraordinary had transpired in that place. They examined the evidence of an event and, in their mind, there was only one explanation. Jesus had risen from the dead! Mary's reported event led to an experience for these two disciples.

John reports that Mary made her way back to the tomb and was once more alone there. For some unknown reason, she apparently refused to enter the tomb and chose rather to bend down and look into it. Her behavior and speech indicated she still had absolutely no clue about the resurrection! Apparently, she had not seen or talked to the two disciples after they visited the tomb and proclaimed Jesus' resurrection.

Still believing that someone had taken the body of Jesus to another place, she wept. Even the presence of two angels and their question to her did nothing to convince her that this was an extraordinary event. In hope of finding some clue to the whereabouts of Jesus' body, she questioned the first "real" person she saw. It seems most unusual for her to disregard the words of two angels but put complete confidence in a total stranger whom she assumed to be only a gardener.

Could it be that Mary was totally consumed with the desire to find the body of Jesus and could not think clearly? For some reason unknown to us, her single mission was to locate his body and she would not be distracted or deterred, even by angels. That persistent search may be difficult for us to understand because it is only a reported event to us. Let it become an experience of searching for our lost loved one and we will better understand her ceaseless effort. Her dogged determination and persistent search lend credence to the fact that this Mary was certainly more than a casual friend. Mary did not recognize Jesus in the resurrected form in which he appeared to her. Could it be that the resurrected Jesus had a different physical appearance than he previously had? Otherwise, Mary would have recognized him immediately.

However, there was instant recognition of him by the manner in which he spoke her name. Another indication of the distinct difference in his physical being is indicated when Mary probably attempted to hug or hold Jesus in some way but was forbidden. That radical difference is also illustrated in other passages in which the resurrected Jesus was not recognized by those who knew him well during his earthly ministry. In most instances, his voice and mannerisms readily revealed who he was.

Satisfied that she had found Jesus, or perhaps that she had been found by Jesus, Mary's feet would not stay still. She raced to the disciples, whomever and wherever they were, and announced to them, "I have seen the Lord!"

This account fails to resolve many issues or answer every question, some of which were noted. Why were there only two disciples to whom Mary first spoke? Why were those two away from the others? Was there some unidentified purpose for the author to write the details of this story as they appear? Were the two disciples present when Mary returned to the tomb? Did they discuss with her what they had discovered? Did those two disciples search for the others and tell them what they had experienced? If they were sure of the Resurrection, why was there no more exuberant response than returning home?

Could it be that John's report on the discovery of the resurrected Jesus had some special purpose for him or someone in the early Christian Church? In spite of the report's differences, its overall emphasis is on the resurrected Jesus. Its format points to the prominence of Peter and may have been intended to justify his leadership role in the early Church.

John's report is greatly clarified and simplified if we delete the digression and difficulty created by reference to the two disciples. Could it be that for some unknown reason to us, that portion of the story has been inappropriately sandwiched between two parts of another reported event. If we delete all references to the two disciples, the story makes good sense from beginning to end and would be more closely aligned with reports found in the other three Gospels. Mary would no longer appear as a dummy, some of her inexplicable behavior would be eliminated and many of our unanswered questions would simply disappear.

Having discovered problems with John's account of Easter and its differences from the other Gospel stories, some people declare all the reports invalid and relegate them to the garbage dump. Could it be they do so because the reported events of Easter are only reported events to them and not experiences for them? All whoi nterpret Easter only as events are inclined to trash the stories related to it.

 Could it be that tucked away in the Easter story is an often overlooked primary clue to human behavior, not only in reference to Easter but also in reference to numerous issues in life? That clue enables us to better understand the normal human response to the world in which we live? It clearly indicates every person responds differently to a reported event than to an experience. One's experience is never the same as the experience of another and can never be rightly expected to elicit an identical response. We mistakenly expect those for whom our experience is only an event to respond as if it were an experience for them. Some hear about events and disregard them. Others hear about events, examine the evidence and experience a definite response to them.

Therefore, the two primary labels for the first Easter, event or experience, are abundantly applicable in our own day. Could it be otherwise?

Anyone who deliberately disregards, denies and improperly names a significant experience may forever suffer adverse effects. Clergy persons, counselors and many others affirm the damage done in the life of those who disregard a deep experience, religious or otherwise. Anyone who seeks to deny, downgrade or disregard a significant experience seemingly sets the stage for more misery in their life.

Could it be that we have yet another clue to human behavior? Some events, but not all, may be disregarded without serious consequences but every deep experience demands conscious examination and a deliberate response. By its very nature, an experience automatically elicits some response. Perhaps we can argue that denial is a response but it is a response fraught with danger. From the Christian perspective, to disregard the reported events and experiences of Easter is detrimental to human potential. This is neither the time nor place to discuss why we respond to reported events and experiences as we do but our response is not altogether accidental, automatic or deliberate. Could the responses to that first Easter have been any different?

John's report indicates Mary's response at the tomb was distinctively different from the two disciples. Though often overlooked, that difference is rather significant and could be yet another clue to our behavior? At the tomb, the two disciples observed and examined the aftermath of an event. the two disciples observed and examined the aftermath of an event. That examination was an experience for them. The surviving evidence of an event became the catalyst for their new experience.

They accepted the validity of a reported event, based on the strong evidence. Mary, on the other hand, was not persuaded by available evidence, even though it seems she had access to it. It took an experience with the risen Christ to convince her that he was alive.

These two responses, accepting evidence and personal experience, are the two major factors that largely determine distinctive changes in life. There is little else to guide us. Each response is vastly different from the other but may ultimately lead us to the same place, as it did for Mary and the two disciples. Depending on the situation, we may rely more on one than the other. A deep experience can truly transform us. Indisputable evidence captures our attention and can lead to a transforming experience. It is difficult to identify where one ends and the other begins. Sometimes, we initially have nothing more than evidence. It is also possible to initially have only an unfamiliar experience which must be examined and analyzed in light of other evidence.

Could it be these two responses describe the normal human process for learning, religious or otherwise? In many minor or serious changes, we did not witness the reported event but we examine the evidence which lead us to a personal experience. We were not involved in the Revolutionary War but we were seriously affected by it. From that event came our country in which we experience democracy. Likewise, we did not witness the life and ministry of Jesus but from him and others came the Christian witness and our religious experiences.

None of us were present that first Easter. We did not experience it. We have limited and incongruent reports of events and experiences from a rather small group of people. We also have some evidence. Our acceptance of the report as valid is an experience in itself but it may also become the catalyst for another experience. Having believed a report, we often deliberately pursue an understanding of it and its possible effect on us. "Believing" is an experience.

Could it be that Easter's events make better sense when we examine them in conjunction with other events prior to and following the resurrection of Jesus? We must examine especially his teachings and actions during the preceding days. What we now call "Holy Week" was especially important in the life and teachings of Jesus. It cannot be safely separated from his total life and ministry or from the Easter experiences.

Careful examination and consideration of reported events and their effect on others may lead to a remarkable experience. All that Jesus said and did during his ministry has some significance for understanding Easter Sunday and what followed. Scholars argue about the content and extent of Jesus' teaching about resurrection in general or his own in particular. Once again, we are not privileged to have the answer. Whatever it was, apparently Jesus said enough to eventually affect the behavior of the disciples, but perhaps only after they examined the evidence and experienced "The Resurrection."

The events and experiences of Easter Sunday were not only a new beginning but they were also the culmination of what had gone before. Without deep appreciation for and some understanding of prior events, Easter Sunday loses its impact, for the original disciples and us. Whatever that first Easter was, evidence indicates it radically transformed a frightened and confused bunch of disciples into a mighty force that rocked the world with their singleness of purpose and indescribable power. The dramatic change in their behavior was reflected in the strength of their conviction. We get the impression that the disciples originally were afraid to declare what they had experienced. They were seemingly embarrassed to speak of it because it was so unusual. They apparently sought some rational explanation for their behavior and experiences.

Something suddenly changed all that. They underwent a life-changing experience! They became emboldened and emphatically proclaimed the resurrection of Jesus. They no longer tried to explain it. Their life-changing experience, whatever it was, transformed them. Their indescribable and radical transformation experience is valid evidence that something happened. Their proclamation became the cornerstone of the Christian gospel preached by the disciples, Paul and many others. They made repeated references to Easter's events and to their own experiences that produced a change in them. They reiterated that the resurrection of Jesus was the reason for their present behavior and forceful proclamation. Evidence of their experience of the event overwhelmed and led others to their own experience with the risen Christ.

The indescribable and new experiences became the motivating force for the remainder of their live. That was true for the original disciples when they first turned aside from their occupations to follow Jesus, even though they did not know where they were going. That conviction guided them when they promised allegiance to his mission and after they failed him. The new experience of a resurrection led to their proclamation that "He is alive" and sustained them when they thought they would soon die. Reported events do not make such radical changes in them or us. Only an experience can do that.

Could it be that the unfolding events of Easter depict the presence of what may be loosely called an individual's Christian religious experience? Even though it is impossible to precisely define, describe or delineate a religious experience, there seems to be some hint of a possible process that repeatedly occurs for those who have a transforming experience.

Those who hear about the events of Easter and do not believe the evidence have no meaningful Christian experience. A vast number of people heard the Easter report immediately after it happened and did not believe. Their lives were not transformed by it. Pilot, the High Priest and other religious and civic leaders took no time to examine the evidence. They seemingly assumed the reported events of Easter were idle tales. Therefore, no transforming experience came to them as an aftermath of these events.

Those who heard the reports, examined their validity and believed, had a transforming religious experience. That process was operative at the first Easter and remains operative today for all who enter the Christian camp. From the Christian perspective, there is no other way to enter. We can never enter by virtue of birth, position, possessions or denominational membership.

Someone may argue that a person could begin their Christian commitment with an experience, not evidence. That may be possible but it seems doubtful. An experience is always set within a context.

As far as we know, transforming religious experiences never occur in a vacuum. If they do, we have no way to understand or interpret them. No person has ever undergone a transforming religious experience, Christian or otherwise, who had not first heard stories and examined some evidence. Like Mary, most, if not all, were searching for something when the experience occurred

A word of caution is necessary when we speak of the presence or absence of a religious transformation process. We must refrain from delineating the exact items that must be believed, the style and manner of the experience or the specific format in which the experience makes itself known. Exact stipulations and specifications imposed by us usurp God's position and make us less than truly Christian. As Christians, we affirm religious transformation is God's business and we have no authority to tell him how he must do it. Every person is different and God deals differently with each of us but there are striking similarities in every transforming experience.

Could it be that we are deeply affected by the Easter story because, by accident or design, it outlines the journey for our own faith experience? It basically duplicates our journey through a life- changing religious experience. We did not witness the ministry of Jesus or his resurrection. Someone first told us the stories, reported the events, and we had to personally examine their validity. Later, we had an experience. We believed. That is very similar to the way it was for the early Christians. They first heard of the events about which others spoke. They examined the evidence for validity. They witnessed the change that occurred in others who believed. What Jesus reportedly said and did resonated with life. Based on what they saw and heard, they were convinced beyond a shadow of doubt that he spoke the truth, that death did not destroy the spirit he embodied and they had experienced his presence. So it is with us.

Like the early disciples, we also believe we have met the risen Christ. Inexplicable experiences led us to that inescapable conclusion. We cannot fully define or describe our experiences but we boldly affirm his spirit is present among us.

We know not exactly how or when it got there but firmly believe it makes a tremendous difference in us. Many of us have some idea when we first recognized its presence. We have no scientific proof for what we believe. We know not where to begin if we try to prove the presence of his spirit, other than to say, "Look at the difference his presence makes in us and others." That is our only proof and that is the basis of our bold proclamation. Our personal experiences in which we "meet Jesus" have similarities to the first Easter experiences and lend credence to those reported events.

As far as we know, Jesus has not appeared to us in a specific bodily form. If he did, like Mary, we did not recognize it was he until later, if at all. Those unknown and informative angels who spoke to us may have first been considered a common occurrence, if not a nuisance.

Like Mary, we may have been busy seeking something so specific, either designated by us or our denomination, we failed to recognize the risen Christ in his new form. We had previously determined what he would look like when he appeared. Later, we recognized the speech, spirit and mannerisms were none other than his, even though they came through unexpected ways, people and places. The overwhelming evidence allowed us to believe nothing else. That which was once only a reported event became a life- changing experience.

We have no complete or individual report of how, when and where each disciple experienced the resurrection of Jesus. Could it have been different for some of them, as the records indicate, just as it was different for some of us? In different ways and at different times they were overwhelmed by the conviction that Jesus was alive. The story of "Doubting Thomas" certainly points to that possibility. They never attempted to describe or explain the exact place and process by which the experience came but they knew they had experienced his living presence. Could it be any different for us?

Like the early followers of Jesus, we heard reports of numerous events. At some point in time, we concluded that those reported events made sense out of life as nothing else could.

Once we truly believed that, we made a commitment to be guided by them. We inexplicably moved from examining reported events to personal experience. We cannot explain the process but we know it happened. He is alive! His spirit permeates us as nothing dead could do. The teachings and behavior of Jesus and other Christians, coupled with his living spirit among us, give meaning and purpose to our lives as nothing else can.

We live in the afterglow of our Easter experience. Even when we fail to faithfully follow, we do not question the validity of the experience. That accepted validity serves as a catalyst for a new one. Easter illustrates failure, forgiveness and fulfillment. The first disciples who failed and fled later returned, found forgiveness and took up their journey with Christ. They knew they failed but they also knew where to start over. When we fail, we too can return, ask for forgiveness and renew our journey with Christ because we do believe.

We fully understand Peter's denial for we are so much like him. We faithfully promise and are pained when we realize we have broken that promise. We are sustained and motivated, even in failure, because we believe. That spirit found in Jesus, or the spirit of Jesus found in us, gives us joy and journeys with us even unto death.

For each of us, Easter is an event or an experience. There is a dramatic difference between the two. Those who see it only as an event can easily relegate it to the religious garbage receptacle. From their perspective, it was an event which had or has no relevance to them.

Those for whom Easter is an experience will never be the same. It must be a continuing experience. Life has been changed and we are no longer what we once were. We cannot fully describe or explain what happened but we know it did. Our best effort is to simply say and show "Jesus is alive" because his spirit lives in us.

CHAPTER ELEVEN
THE HOLY SPIRIT
Genesis 2:7-9, Acts 2:1-4, Galatians 5:16-25
Genesis

7: then the LORD God formed man of dust from the ground, and breathed into his nostrils the breath of life; and man became a living being.

8: And the LORD God planted a garden in Eden, in the east; and there he put the man whom he had formed.

9: And out of the ground the LORD God made to grow every tree that is pleasant to the sight and good for food, the tree of life also in the midst of the garden, and the tree of the knowledge of good and evil.
Acts

1: When the day of Pentecost had come, they were all together in one place.

2: And suddenly a sound came from heaven like the rush of a mighty wind, and it filled all the house where they were sitting.

3: And there appeared to them tongues as of fire, distributed and resting on each one of them.

4: And they were all filled with the Holy Spirit and began to speak in other tongues, as the Spirit gave them utterance.
Galatians

16: But I say, walk by the Spirit, and do not gratify the desires of the flesh.

17: For the desires of the flesh are against the Spirit, and the desires of the Spirit are against the flesh; for these are opposed to each other, to prevent you from doing what you would.

18: But if you are led by the Spirit you are not under the law.

19: Now the works of the flesh are plain: fornication, impurity, licentiousness,

20: idolatry, sorcery, enmity, strife, jealousy, anger, selfishness, dissension, party spirit,

21: envy, drunkenness, carousing, and the like. I warn you, as I warned you before, that those who do such things shall not inherit the kingdom of God.

22: But the fruit of the Spirit is love, joy, peace, patience, kindness, goodness, faithfulness,

23: gentleness, self-control; against such there is no law.

24: And those who belong to Christ Jesus have crucified the flesh with its passions and desires.

25: If we live by the Spirit, let us also walk by the Spirit.

No mortal can adequately define, completely describe or fully understand the Holy Spirit. The inability to do so causes some people to have little or no concern for it and to relegate all scriptural references to the religious garbage dump. Some among us believe biblical references to it further emphasize God's favoritism in one- time events for special people in special places and circumstances. If true, they say, it cannot be explained or justified. Are they saying something is acceptable only if we can understand, explain or justify it?

If our ability to understand, describe or explain something is the only criteria applied in judging its validity, little remains worthy of our thoughts and actions. I do not know about you but I do not fully understand myself and most of the things around me, including electricity, computers, telephones, automobiles, radios, space, my wife, my children, other people, God, the Holy Spirit, love, and much more.

In fact, there is nothing that I fully understand or am able to perfectly describe or define. That does not mean I deny their existence, refuse to accept and appreciate them or that I relegate them to the garbage dump. Their mysteries intrigue and entice me toward better understanding. What I don't know about them might hurt me! Even though I am aware I will never fully understand any of them, I desire to know and appreciate all of them to the best of my ability. Partial knowledge and understanding are far more rewarding than trashing anything.

Could it be that some refuse to ponder the Holy Spirit because they believe it deals primarily with divine magic and bodiless heavenly beings called "holy ghosts?" Having never seen such a being, they doubt their existence. Most likely, they also hope they will never see one! They focus primarily on stories of ghosts who, suddenly, unexpectedly and reportedly appeared under unusual circumstances. Scary childhood stories left indelible marks that were not jettisoned with youth. "Ghost stories", past or present, stir up more anxiety than they have the desire or ability to confront. Those persons harbor an erroneous idea implanted early in life by others who meant no harm. Ignorance and fear provide them a favorable framework to renounce the Holy Spirit's relevance and relegate it to the religious garbage dump.

Could it be that some of us seldom speak of the Holy Spirit simply because we do not know what to say or believe? We are reasonably certain it is worthy of consideration and vital to our religious life. Religious leaders and ordinary Christians convinced us of its importance. We have heard many confusing and conflicting statements made by people acting as if they were the only ones who received the correct revelation form God. Some of their pronouncements do not mesh with other things we hold true. Such contradictions, whether made by one person or many, cannot all be true and they puzzled us. In order to cover our misgivings and lack of personal clarity, we often avoid the subject. Avoidance of the subject may also reflect our fear of what God will do to us if we are incorrect and incomplete.

Could it be that some of us seldom speak about the Holy Spirit because we aren't sure if that subject stands alone or if it is connected to or encompasses the Holy Ghost, God's spirit, God's presence, the unseen action of God, etc.? We are often reluctant, if not afraid, to voice our opinion on religious matters until we have at least some vague idea of how it relates to other important issues.

Any successful effort to avoid the subject reduces the chance of exposing our lack of clarity. Apparently, some of us subscribe to the philosophy that it is better to let others question our knowledge than to open our mouth and remove all doubt.

Could it be that we are consciously aware of our failure to fully develop the divine essence within and are therefore reluctant to talk and read about the Holy Spirit? If we fit that category, we want to keep it out of sight and out of mind. This is especially true if we turned away from previous religious promises or are reluctant to maintain Christian behavior. Any reminder of that failure or a call to renew those promises can cause great pain. Reading and talking about the Holy Spirit disturbs our status quo and we don't like to be disturbed because it can be painful.

Could we have an unconscious need to cultivate that inner spirit because we were designed with an innate hunger to cooperate with the Holy Spirit? Even though we may not intellectually know what the hunger is, we usually know when it is unmet. Given the conditions in our macho world and our desire to fit in it, we dare not admit to any inner and unmet hunger because we and others consider that a weakness. Hearing the clarion call of other prominent "spirits," we refuse to recognize our deep inner hunger and continue to feed, perhaps gorge, ourselves on that which can never fully satisfy. In spite of a lingering emptiness and a meaningless life, some individuals quickly renounce any suggestion that worldly spirits are insufficient to fully satisfy all basic human needs. Any suggestion that they are incorrect bothers them and they do not want to be bothered by any reminder of that possibility.

Some among us believe that talk of an inner religious hunger is old fashioned, non-intellectual and totally unnecessary. Vehement denial may be strong proof of its existence!

Having indicated some of the diverse difficulties we face, could it be that the Holy Spirit is totally beyond any human insight or comprehension? Since it is so confusing and we have so few absolute facts, is it religiously correct to avoid thoughts and conversations about it? I think not. Complete knowledge is impossible but partial knowledge enables us to participate more fully in a meaningful life. Lack of total knowledge does not keep us from using the phone, automobile, e-mail, etc. A greater knowledge of them enhances life's experiences.

Why should we make a distinction when we consider the Holy Spirit? Inability to acquire complete knowledge does not negate our ability to attain partial knowledge. Since the Holy Spirit is a vital part of our Christian faith and life, we diligently seek a better understanding of it, believing God has made partial understanding possible and available.

Even though we correctly crave a more complete understanding of the Holy Spirit, that may not be as urgent as we first assumed. Christianity affirms that salvation is through faith, not knowledge. Complete understanding of the Holy Spirit, God, etc. is not the criteria for our salvation. If so, none of us would have it. This does not deny or diminish the importance of knowledge but simply puts it in the proper perspective in reference to salvation. Knowledge definitely augments genuine Christian living, even though our understanding may be only partial. Faith is primary for our salvation but knowledge facilitates proper and purposeful demonstration of that faith in our daily life. Faith without intellectual application often leads to unwise, unhealthy and unholy behavior. Everyone who seeks to be genuinely Christian has, to some degree, contemplated the Holy Spirit and its meaning for themselves and others. Noted theologians, prominent preachers and ordinary people have expressed their thoughts on the subject. Numerous pages of religious literature contain some of their profound thoughts collected over centuries.

After all that others have said and done, some of us remain unsatisfied and seek more insight.

I struggled for years to find an understanding of the Holy Spirit that made sense without relegating it to the realm of divine magic and impenetrable mystery. The above reasons for refusal to talk about the Holy Spirit came from conversations with and observations of others. I am indebted to scholarly writings, teachers, preachers and ordinary people whose insights affected my own. Having read and heard extensive comments on the Holy Spirit, I remained unsatisfied until I developed a personal approach to it. Logic and my understanding of religious faith tell me this is also true for everyone.

Could it be that our best insight into the Holy Spirit must always come through deep personal experiences? There is a distinct difference between an intellectual understanding and an understanding that comes through an experience. Much that we know never came exclusively from another.

Intellectually, we know it hurts when a door is slammed on your finger but to experience it is an enlightening and educational process. We learn about the Holy Spirit from others but there can be no substitute for personal experience. However, personal experiences are affected by intelligence.

We understand the Holy Spirit, to the best of our ability, only after we have knowingly experienced it. Apparently, it is never a cookie-cutter experience precisely reproduced on every occurrence. Here is a clue to why we have difficulty in providing an exact description or definition. Some have no experience and others have slightly different experiences.Even though the Holy Spirit is beyond definition, there are descriptive words and identifiable parameters that enable serious thought and discussion. There are usable metaphors and similes suitable for further understanding, but they are always imperfect and incomplete. There are some handles, some recognizable aspects, to grasp while we search for more meaning.

Scripture, scholars and saints gave us some help at this point, but they also struggled in their efforts to fully understand, describe and explain.

Our personal struggle is similar to theirs, if not a continuation of it. I, and many devout Christians, have little knowledge of the original languages in which ancient writings and the Bible first appeared. I also have no easy access to the oral traditions and social customs that preserved the words until written. That knowledge is crucial to understanding the Bible, any subject in it and especially its words about the Holy Spirit.

My understanding of the original texts and oral tradition is limited primarily to what others tell me. Since translators and interpreters were numerous, diverse, only human and occasionally more interested in "translating" than in accuracy, their translations and interpretations may contain imperfections. They, like all of us, often began with some bias that undoubtedly shaded everything they said. If their translations and interpretations are occasionally or partially incorrect, I have an additional hurdle to negotiate. My understanding of the English texts is predicated not only on what they say but also on my bias and my efforts to understand and interpret them.

Could it be that basic lessons learned early in English classes are extremely helpful in understanding comments from others and our own thoughts on the Holy Spirit? We were taught that words are very important. They have meaning and convey thoughts.

Why should we make a distinction when we consider the Holy Spirit? Inability to acquire complete knowledge does not negate our ability to attain partial knowledge. Since the Holy Spirit is a vital part of our Christian faith and life, we diligently seek a better understanding of it, believing God has made partial understanding possible and available. Even though we correctly crave a more complete understanding of the Holy Spirit, that may not be as urgent as we first assumed. Christianity affirms that salvation is through faith, not knowledge.

Complete understanding of the Holy Spirit, God, etc. is not the criteria for our salvation. If so, none of us would have it. This does not deny or diminish the importance of knowledge but simply puts it in the proper perspective in reference to salvation. Knowledge definitely augments genuine Christian living, even though our understanding may be only partial. Faith is primary for our salvation but knowledge facilitates proper and purposeful demonstration of that faith in our daily life. Faith without intellectual application often leads to unwise, unhealthy and unholy behavior.

Everyone who seeks to be genuinely Christian has, to some degree, contemplated the Holy Spirit and its meaning for themselves and others. Noted theologians, prominent preachers and ordinary people have expressed their thoughts on the subject. Numerous pages of religious literature contain some of their profound thoughts collected over centuries. After all that others have said and done, some of us remain unsatisfied and seek more insight.

I struggled for years to find an understanding of the Holy Spirit that made sense without relegating it to the realm of divine magic and impenetrable mystery. The above reasons for refusal to talk about the Holy Spirit came from conversations with and observations of others. I am indebted to scholarly writings, teachers, preachers and ordinary people whose insights affected my own. Having read and heard extensive comments on the Holy Spirit, I remained unsatisfied until I developed a personal approach to it. Logic and my understanding of religious faith tell me this is also true for everyone.

Could it be that our best insight into the Holy Spirit must always come through deep personal experiences? There is a distinct difference between an intellectual understanding and an understanding that comes through an experience. Much that we know never came exclusively from another. Intellectually, we know it hurts when a door is slammed on your finger but to experience it is an enlightening and educational process. We learn about the Holy Spirit from others but there can be no substitute for personal experience. However, personal experiences are affected by intelligence.

We understand the Holy Spirit, to the best of our ability, only after we have knowingly experienced it. Apparently, it is never a cookie-cutter experience precisely reproduced on every occurrence. Here is a clue to why we have difficulty in providing an exact description or definition. Some have no experience and others have slightly different experiences.

 Even though the Holy Spirit is beyond definition, there are descriptive words and identifiable parameters that enable serious thought and discussion. There are usable metaphors and similes suitable for further understanding, but they are always imperfect and incomplete. There are some handles, some recognizable aspects, to grasp while we search for more meaning. Scripture, scholars and saints gave us some help at this point, but they also struggled in their efforts to fully understand, describe and explain.

Our personal struggle is similar to theirs, if not a continuation of it. I, and many devout Christians, have little knowledge of the original languages in which ancient writings and the Bible first appeared. I also have no easy access to the oral traditions and social customs that preserved the words until written. That knowledge is crucial to understanding the Bible, any subject in it and especially its words about the Holy Spirit.

My understanding of the original texts and oral tradition is limited primarily to what others tell me. Since translators and interpreters were numerous, diverse, only human and occasionally more interested in "translating" than in accuracy, their translations and interpretations may contain imperfections. They, like all of us, often began with some bias that undoubtedly shaded everything they said. If their translations and interpretations are occasionally or partially incorrect, I have an additional hurdle to negotiate. My understanding of the English texts is predicated not only on what they say but also on my bias and my efforts to understand and interpret them.

Could it be that basic lessons learned early in English classes are extremely helpful in understanding comments from others and our own thoughts on the Holy Spirit? We were taught that words are very important. They have meaning and convey thoughts.

They produce a context and provide parameters for the discussion. By definition, they include some things and exclude others. Words are like building blocks. They are designed to be joined together in order to create something greater than themselves. If we know and focus on the meaning of words, we are able to formulate and communicate complicated ideas by combining simple ones.

The two words, "Holy Spirit," deserve careful and individual examination that may enable us to build a better understanding of them when combined. A clear understanding of them provides parameters within which we discover and discuss penetrating insights into this tantalizing subject. "Holy" is a distinctively religious word found numerous times in Judeo-Christian literature. Its use also abounds in many other religious traditions. It is always a religious word with some connection to deity. Anything designated as holy is consistently above the ordinary. When used to describe anything physical and human, it usually indicates special qualities, characteristics, etc., often bestowed by a divine being.

The Biblical stories of creation, Christ and Christendom repeatedly emphasize that aspect of its meaning. God is certainly far above and beyond ordinary human beings. However, he seeks to enhance their existence by imparting to them some of his likeness. Anything set aside by God for his special use is labeled "holy." Old Testament Patriarchs, prophets and priests repeatedly used "holy" as a preface for persons, places, things and actions. They speak of holy mountains, holy ground, holy places of worship, holy people, etc. Their connection to God, regardless of how, makes them holy. In the Old Testament, that which is holy deserves awe and reverence,f requently being the object of worship. Writers of the New Testament maintain a similar emphasis. Scripture is saturated with illustrations.

In the Greek translation of the New Testament, the root word for "holy" is closely related to the word for saint. At some point in time, it signified that which was set apart for the special purpose of worship. The ancient Greeks used it with specific reference to something of awe and reverence.

Later, it came to signify that which was clean and uncontaminated. It often appears in conjunction with words like spirit, place, a deity, saint, etc.

Throughout the Bible and the Judeo-Christian community, "Holy" almost always signifies that which is above the ordinary, set apart for a special purpose and directly connected to God who is the source of all that is holy.

"Spirit" is the second small and power-packed word deserving special attention. In the ancient Hebrew language, it sometimes meant breath, soul or heart. The Old Testament writers used it to describe God's person, presence and performance. When the spirit moved, God acted. "Spirit" was used in various ways to reflect different manifestations of God. In the creation story, God's spirit was at work. He breathed, infused, his spirit into humanity. His spirit not only gave life but it also maintained and protected that which he created, from the first person to a special nation and then to a special revelation of himself. The spirit of God, the essence of his being, created, moved, guided, protected, etc. in almost every major story of both Testaments. His active spirit has nothing to do with magic. It is a natural part of who he is and what he does.

According to the Creation story, each person has an unidentifiable element called "spirit." In contrast to the spirit in us, we have a physical body. We can argue that the spirit is not just in us but it is us and it has a body! The kind of spirit we possess, or that possesses us, basically dictates our behavior. Adam and Eve illustrated thatf act. Without stretching it too far, their story provides a preview of what it took many years for us to recognize. Our true inner spirit is indicated and demonstrated in ordinary behavior, i.e., love, anger, kindness, trust, generosity, etc.

(Ref. Gal 5:16-24) In the final analysis, the spirit in us is far more important than the physical body in which it dwells. We have, or are, an indescribable essence that lacks measurable dimensions. At least to some degree, we choose whether our dominant inner spirit is good or evil. There are only imperfect outside indicators of what spirit is inside, but the aftermath of our action provides a clear clue.

The Creation story indicates indescribable and immeasurable spirits are also loose in the world. They are reflected in two ways, either as a good spirit or as an evil spirit. Each spirit is readily available to us. We must choose the one with which we normally associate, and that choice dictates the primary spirit reflected in our life. The story of Adam and Eve in The Garden speaks precisely to this point.

God's spirit is distinctively different from any other spirit, especially an evil spirit of an ungodly nature. The Bible portrays God's active and unseen spirit seeking to communicate with our unseen spirit, enabling our primary spirit to be an imitation of his. That action began with creation, continued throughout biblical times, brought Christianity into existence, and will continue until the end of time. Apparently, God intends for us to be complete only when the dominant spirit in us imitates his spirit. In my book, A Pain In The Gut, I discuss the subject of good and evil spirits available to each of us. The gist of that discussion is applicable here. Could it be that God's image implanted in us is the ability to love and that we must love something in some way? If love best describes who God is and what he does, perhaps love also best describes who we are and what we do. The nature of God and us necessitates loving (valuing) something. Our only choice is to love either appropriately or inappropriately. Appropriate love is God-like and good but inappropriate love is idolatry and evil. Whatever we love the most is our "god." It controls us and generates a particular spirit, an immeasurable dimension we reflect in our behavior.

The good and God-like spirit we call "Holy Spirit" but all else we call evil. The New Testament writers seemingly accept without question the Old Testament understanding of "spirit." In the Gospels, Jesus frequently refers to the ancient Jewish teachings about God's spirit.

Paul talks about the work of the Spirit and sometimes connects his comments to ancient Jewish ideas. The early Christian Church attributes its survival and growth to the unseen and active spirit of God. Even though Old Testament writers often spoke of the spirit of God and God's unseen action, it was a New Testament writer who added a new insight when he described God as "Spirit" in John 4:24. If anyone previously thought of God in this manner, this seems to be the first written record of that insight.

In the original Greek version of the New Testament, the word "spirit" comes from the root word meaning a "sudden blast," "movement of air," "a blowing action," and "breath." Our English word "pneumatic," powered by air, is also derived from the same root word. When the New Testament writers speak of God's spirit in action, they often use words associated with "wind" to describe it.

If God's spirit is similar to the wind, we know something about it because we know something about the wind. We have personally experienced it. It has no physical form or visible dimensions. It may be anticipated but it is never guaranteed. It comes according to its own time and not at our request. No mortal can be sure when or if it will demonstrate its presence. Its time of arrival, direction of travel, length of stay, and ultimate results are unpredictable. We cannot see it coming and often recognize its presence and power only after it is gone. It announces its presence by activity over which we have little or no control. It may come and go without our awareness. It may come as a very gentle breeze or as a mighty blast. Its effect may or may not be immediately recognized and may even be inappropriately called something else. It is almost always viewed as ordinary action.

The above characteristics of the wind are applicable to God's Spirit. It is God's unseen action operating in various degrees and places, perhaps without our request or knowledge and commonly called ordinary. Partial awareness of the wind's behavior does not completely disclose or fully describe the Holy Spirit but such knowledge enables recognition of its presence and some of its characteristics.

Someone may ask if the destructive nature of the wind can be likened to any action of the Spirit. Does the analogy break down at this point? The answer depends on what you believe about many other things.

Could it be that the analogy holds even here? When the Holy Spirit forcefully moves against evil spirits and triumphs, something gets defeated and destroyed. Prior to destruction, the Holy Spirit disturbs and provides stiff opposition to evil. Destruction may not be desired by God but those who refuse to participate with the Holy Spirit inadvertently choose their own destruction. The Spirit works to destroy evil and thereby has a destructive element, like the wind. The Holy Spirit's destructive element is never designed for evil but only and always for ultimate good.

The New Testament writers spent little effort defining the Spirit of God but provide numerous reports on its various activities. The ordinary people of that day understood the meaning of spirit, perhaps better than we. We likely assume their understanding was less than ours. Intellectually speaking, that argument may have some merit but probably lacks strong support from the experience level. They freely spoke of it and readily gave credence to it.

Their lack of knowledge was both a blessing and a curse. For them, "spirit" had the same characteristic as it did in the Old Testament, without identifiable dimension and could be good or evil. God was the source of everything good and holy. Indescribable and inexplicable events were most often attributed to God's action. In the eyes of the New Testament writers, God's spirit worked through Jesus and the early Christians to facilitate the Spirit's duplication in the lives of ordinary people, making them no longer just ordinary but set apart for God's special purpose. A broad knowledge of these two words, "holy" and "spirit," enhances our understanding of "the Holy Spirit." The combined meaning of these two words, and all their ramifications, sharpens our focus on the Spirit's nature and action. It is God's active and loving presence moving among his creation for his purposes. It is the essence of God that has no measurable or physical dimensions. Wherever and whenever God acts, his spirit, the Holy Spirit, is there.

If God is active in a particular time, place or event, his spirit is there. Therefore, the Holy Spirit is the unseen presence and power of God in action, seeking to cleanse, renew and set apart some portion of his creation for his specific purpose. It is always a good spirit and always acts for God's good purposes. It is holy because it is a part of God and therefore deserves awe and reverence from us. It is spirit because, like the wind, it is invisible, immeasurable and powerful, but whose existence is often surmised only by its aftermath. From creation to the present, different people used different words to symbolize similar things. Specific words often reflected a particular time, place or religious custom. In speaking of the presence of God in action, some use Holy Spirit, Holy Ghost, the spirit of God, the presence of God, the breath of God, Paraclete, Comforter, Counselor, and others. Most modern Christians seemingly prefer "Holy Spirit" as their verbiage to symbolize the presence of God in action. It is synonymous with other similar words and can usually be freely interchanged with any of them. Different words may be more descriptive of a particular action but they always speak of God's nature, action and unseen presence.

If we can correctly say the Holy Spirit is the presence of God in action, we may have to rethink at least one of our long held religious ideas. For many reasons and through various ways, some of us originally thought the Holy Spirit made its first appearance in New Testament time. If so, it is in name only. Numerous New Testament passages refer, in one way or another, to the "coming of the Spirit" or some future manifestation of it and thereby may contribute to that erroneous assumption. Perhaps that assumption is made because too many professing Christians know too little about the Holy Spirit and the Old Testament! If we think the Holy Spirit made its initial appearance in the New Testament, we have serious problems. If it first appeared there, how do we speak about God's prior action?

If we find another name for that action and give it an individual identity, what does that do for our understanding of the Trinity? If we give God's Old Testament action a name other than one synonymous with the Holy Spirit, does that mean we have two names for the same thing? Did God act differently prior to the coming of Christ?

If we argue that the Holy Spirit first appears in the New Testament, we must give some other interpretive word for God's active presence in the Old Testament.

A new look at some Biblical passages may help remove erroneous assumptions about the Holy Spirit. A brief passage from one of the creation accounts, located in Genesis 2:7, speaks of God infusing the breath of life into the first humans whom he formed from dust. Genesis 41:38, Exodus 31:3, Numbers 24:2, Judges 3:10 and numerous other Old Testament passages refer to the spirit of God being upon and within certain people.

Numerous other Old Testament passages repeatedly tell of God's spirit moving to accomplish his purposes. His active spirit brought into being a chosen people, set them aside for a special purpose and led them to a promised land. The Old Testament can be best summarized as stories of God's spirit working with his people; creating, calling and enabling them to imitate his essence of goodness and love implanted in them at creation. The spirit of God at work in the New Testament is identical to God's spirit at work in the Old Testament. It was active before the birth of Christ. Matthew 1:18-25 and Luke 1:26-38 provide portions from the birth stories of Jesus. Each account specifically identifies the Holy Spirit as the primary actor in the mysterious and holy event. Luke's account of the infant Jesus' obligatory temple visit (Luke 2:25-32) tells about Simeon, an old and righteous man "filled with the Holy Spirit." Mark 1:9-12 tells us that "the Spirit" descended on Jesus at his baptism and immediately thereafter Jesus was driven by "the Spirit" into the wilderness. Matthew reports that as Jesus came out of the water following his baptism, Jesus saw the "Spirit of God descending like a dove and alighting on him." (3:16) John uses very similar words when he describes the baptism of Jesus, saying, "I saw the Spirit descending from heaven like a dove." (John 1:32) According to Luke 4:18, Jesus was in the synagogue and read from Isaiah, "The spirit of the Lord is upon me......" Luke 10:21 says that Jesus rejoiced in the Holy Spirit. Jesus made reference to the Holy Spirit in Mark 12:36 when he said "By the Holy spirit" David received and followed instructions from the Lord.

The above-mentioned New Testament passages, along with others, reflect an irrefutable acceptance of the Holy Spirit's activity in the birth, life and ministry of Jesus prior to his resurrection. It was present and active before Jesus' birth and immediately thereafter. The people of that time either believed the Holy Spirit was active prior to and in the birth and life of Jesus or story tellers and writers injected that belief at a later time. There seems to be no other choice. We have evidence where writers tampered with the original stories but not these. Evidence indicates participants in these stories believed the Holy Spirit was present and active from creation onward. Could it be that disregard for or ignorance of biblical material cause some people to assume the Holy Spirit originated after Jesus' death and in the Christian community? A misunderstanding and misinterpretation of a few verses in the Gospel of John contributes to that erroneous assumption. John has Jesus declare, in 14:16, that "I will pray the Father and he will give you another Counselor." Immediately thereafter, in verse 26, Jesus declares that he who will come to them is the Holy Spirit. Later, in 15:26, Jesus said, "When the Counselor comes, whom I will send to you from the father…. he will bear witness to me." In John 16:7, we read, "If I do not go away, the Counselor will not come to you, but if I go, I will send him to you." Based exclusively on these passages, anyone with more enthusiasm than understanding may easily conclude that Jesus is the predecessor of the Holy Spirit and Jesus will send it when Jesus chooses. Upon careful study, these passages say that only if one wants them to say it. The fact that Jesus will ask the Father to send the Counselor to the disciples at some future time does not necessarily mean the Counselor is absent or nonexistent. The fact that it will come in the future does not say it is not here now.

Could it be this is a prayer by Jesus for the disciples' enlightenment, a prayer that they will understand in the future even though they did not understand then? Jesus offers them reassurance of God's continuous presence. God is here and he will also be present in the future. Was Jesus politely telling them they will one day experience God's presence as never before, if they remain faithful? Could it be that Jesus tells them, and us, gradual growth is a natural part of spiritual development?

By its very nature, the Spirit will come again in the future, as it did in the past, to all who remain faithful. We do not get all it has to offer at once! Seasoned saints should understand more than infant Christians.

Jesus seldom prayed for God to be active among the disciples because he knew God would automatically do that. That is God's nature. Rather, Jesus prayed that the disciples would recognize God's active presence and then willingly respond to it. Jesus prayed that the Disciples would favorably respond to the presently available Spirit, not that the Spirit would later make itself available to the disciples. It was already there. Up to this point, all the bulbs in the disciples' chandelier were not burning brightly! Jesus therefore prays for their enlightenment. Jesus' stated necessity for his departure from the disciples could mean they had not learned to follow the Holy Spirit because they depended too much on the physical presence of Jesus. Jesus' departure was not necessary for the Spirit to arrive but necessary for the disciples to accomplish a higher level of understanding. This is a fundamental lesson for life because disciples, students, children and everyone must move beyond the shadow of their leader in order to reach a higher level of life. Jesus was no dummy and this statement reflects his understanding about his disciples and life in general. The Gospel of John adds additional dilemma to the origin of the Holy Spirit. In his post-resurrection account, chapter 20, John reports the frightened disciples were gathered behind locked doors and Jesus suddenly appeared among them. After their recognition of him, in verse 22, John says Jesus "breathed on them" and then said specifically to them, "Receive the Holy Spirit.

" Why should we assume it has to be a new gift to them? Did Jesus mean, "Receive the Holy Spirit again?" He may have used those exact words on other occasions. Could Jesus actually mean, "Become more aware of the Holy Spirit?" Perhaps he said in no uncertain words, "Your guiding spirit must now be Christ-like love, the Holy Spirit, because I can remain no longer with you."

Could this be John's way of telling a "new creation story" modeled in some measure after the first one? The disciples could become "new beings" with a divine purpose only if they were filled with the Holy Spirit. Just because the disciples received an infusion of the Holy Spirit has nothing to do with the time of its origin nor does it indicate its total absence from them prior to this experience. This report is more about Jesus' concern for and the condition of the disciples than the Holy Spirit. Someone may think the opening verses of the second chapter of Acts supports the notion that the Holy Spirit first appeared in New Testament times. It tells the fascinating story about the day of Pentecost. If that is the only biblical story we heard or remembered, we might assume no other record indicated a similar occurrence in which the Spirit's activity was readily recognized or widespread. Perhaps we should reconsider some Old Testament stories in which vast numbers of people had transforming religious experiences. Verses two through four, in Acts 2, describe the experience of Pentecost but they do not indicate or insinuate this is the original appearance of the Holy Spirit.

Note the verbiage in Acts 2, when it states that something "like the rush of a violent wind" came from heaven. It further states that many in attendance were "filled with the Holy Spirit" and afterwards some of them engaged in unusual speech recognized even by foreigners who did not normally understand another language. "Speaking in other languages" provides insight into the effects of the Holy Spirit, not its origin. If the essence of the Holy Spirit is love, those who were unquestionably filled with love demonstrated it in such a fashion that all could see the motive behind their behavior. The spirit of Christ-like love speaks a universal language easily understood by almost everyone. Many of those present may have been "baptized with the Spirit" and the awareness of that presence may have been a new experience for them. Christlike love became the new guide for their lives. That does not mean the Spirit's existence is new. It was new only to them. That wonderful, new and transforming religious experience in no way marks the birth of the Holy Spirit.

Pentecost depicts the Holy Spirit in action at a particular place and in a different setting. It may be considered a partial fulfillment of a promise made by Jesus but it is the same active spirit of God, present with Jesus and active since creation. Peter's sermon at Pentecost, Acts 2: 17 & 18, points to the words of the prophet Joel and makes it quite clear he connects the present action of the Spirit with God's active presence in the Old Testament.

The most prolific writer of the New Testament, Paul, said more about the "Spirit" than any other writer. For him, the Spirit is from heaven as an act of God's love (I Thes. 4:8). Paul repeatedly connected the Spirit's activity to events in human history. He borrows from the creation story and emphasizes the distinctive difference between flesh and spirit, or physical and spiritual. Paul believes the disobedience of Adam was set right in the obedience of Christ who enables our controlling spirit to be restored to that intended by God in creation. Paul's writings encompass specific instructions and encouragement for others to live under the direction of the Holy Spirit, first through conversion and then by bearing "good fruit."

According to Paul, the divine Spirit is readily available to all who will receive it. The resurrection of Jesus, Pentecost, Paul's conversion, the conversion of those to whom Paul preached and daily Christian living primarily resulted from the work of the Holy Spirit. For Paul, that action of the Spirit was a continuation of God's active spirit throughout human history.

For Paul, everyone was created with the potential to be dominated by either a good or evil spirit, as indicated in the creation story. These spirits do not appear to enter and depart through a physical process. The potential for both are always present. Paul emphasizes our responsibility to decide which spirit will dominate. Spirits are not disconnected entities roaming about in search of a dwelling. The potential for either dwells in us, first by creation and then gains control by invitation and cooperation. Every dominant spirit in one's life, whether evil or good, declares its presence by the fruits of one's behavior.

Paul specifically addresses this matter in Galatians 5:16-26. He calls us to "live by the Spirit" and then explains what that entails. For those who are "led by the Spirit," certain behaviors are forbidden and others are mandatory.

Forbidden behavior includes idolatry, fornication, strife, jealousy, envy, anger, drunkenness, pride, etc. (Gal. 5:19-21). Each forbidden action reflects the presence of an evil,

unhealthy and unholy spirit. The "fruit of the Spirit is love, joy, peace, patience, kindness, generosity, faithfulness, gentleness and self-control." (Gal. 5:22-23) Every enumerated "fruit", good or evil, reflects a person's dominant spirit.

Paul's list of forbidden and required behaviors poses a problem if we make it all inclusive or the only measure by which we judge all behavior. His list is incomplete so we must categorize all remaining possible behavior as originating from a good or evil spirit. Our inability to properly judge or to know the extenuating circumstances prohibits valid judgment. Specific behavior under one situation may be less than good but under another condition it may be very appropriate. Therefore, if we seek to live according to the Spirit, our judgment on the behavior of others should be infrequent, temporary and with trepidation. Certain behavior definitely indicates one's basic spirit but hasty and harsh judgment may once again be contrary to the Holy Spirit working in us.

If we take Paul's words seriously, living in tune with the Holy Spirit may be more mundane than many would have us believe. It is a lifestyle readily available, from creation to the present, to all who choose it. It first requires a conscious acceptance of the invitation to imitate God's spirit, best illustrated and demonstrated in Jesus. It requires a conscious effort to always act according to that spirit, to live under the guidance of Christ-like love. All behavior must demonstrate the spirit of that divine love. Living in tune with the Spirit requires no specialized equipment, specific location, or stipulated clientele.

That spirit of divine love motivates every genuine effort to relieve heartache and suffering, even if it is only a cup of cool water to a thirsty traveler, food for the hungry, shelter for the homeless, etc. It is active in the comforting and kind words to the bereaved, lonely or distressed. It is in every act of Christ-like love expressed in word or deed to family, friend or foe. It affects the way we treat our mate, our children, our neighbors, our pets and our possessions. It has something to say about what automobile we drive and the way we drive it, what we do with our trash, how we treat the environment, etc. Its presence is reflected in our use of time, talents, and possessions. Life in tune with the Holy Spirit transforms everyday existence into meaningful and joyful living.

It enlarges the spirit of goodness with which we were endowed at our creation, enabling us to overcome evil temptations
and to fulfill God's intended purpose. Christ-like living is no self-serving outer garment that we wear at will but rather it is a reflection of who we really are and the spirit that dominates us.
Could it be that the Spirit always acts first in the small things so that it may eventually accomplish greater things? Our willingness to trust more completely and our ability to respond more appropriately enhance the growth process. In our physical life, we crawl before we walk and we vigorously exercise to enable endurance. Why should it be different in participating with the Spirit? Dedication, discipline and experience enhance wider applications of the Spirit's leadership even in mundane activities.

Could it be that the ancient writers of the creation story were factually correct and far more profound than some of us first thought? God implanted into each human being a portion of his indefinable and immeasurable spirit, thereby sharing with us his image and his essence. Therefore, our basic human element is more spiritual than physical. The true measure of whom and what we are is the dominating spirit that dwells within us. Could it be that we find the full meaning of our existence only when we consciously develop that good spirit of love and when we live in keeping with it? This interpretation certainly permeates the basic biblical messages from beginning to end.

The potential to be directed by an evil spirit always remains within us. The creation story hints at that and our human experiences validate it. We constantly struggle to distinguish between good or evil, no matter how committed we are to the spirit of love. Evil spirits surreptitiously and openly tempt us with pleasure and promise. Could it be that? God made us similar to the tree referred to in Genesis 2:9. That one tree in the center of the Garden had elements of both good and evil. Its fruits were consumable. Could we transpose the idea and consider the core of our being somewhat like that tree? Each occupies the center spot and each can produce good or evil. Even as Adam and Eve had a choice of which fruit to eat, we must also decide whether good or evil will dominate us. Carelessly partaking of the forbidden fruit, from the tree or the self-centeredness, may enable existence but only the good fruit produces a good spirit. The potential to change what controls us is part of our God-given nature, infused at creation. Living in tune with the Holy Spirit does not destroy our potential for evil but it does keep us on the positive side.

The more dedicated we are to living in tune with the Spirit and the more experience we have in that kind of living, the less likely we are to deliberately choose an opposite lifestyle. As any good Methodist would affirm, we are expected to "grow in grace" but we must remember we can also "fall from grace." If not, at some point we claim perfection and no one other than God is perfect.

If we live in the presence of good spirits, we are enabled to imitate them. If the "less than good spirits" surround us, we are more likely to partake of improper "fruit" and behave accordingly. If our early developmental diet provided by others was good fruit, we were blessed. If it was primarily improper food, we tended to develop "evil spirits" of selfishness, greed, anger, hatred, etc. The spirit that dominates us seems to multiply and increase its strength while diminishing the strength of its opposite. Those firmly committed to Christ-like love willingly seek its additional influence. When the evil spirits become selfishly entrenched, any encroaching good spirit meets resistance, as illustrated in the stories where Jesus offered help to those controlled by evil spirits.

Christians are aware of the Holy Spirit's active presence, welcome it into their lives and endeavor to live in keeping with it. Christian conversion is consciously saying a joyful "yes" to the spirit's offer to guide us and set us apart for its use.

Christian living is our deliberate endeavor to always act in harmony with the divine spirit in us. Maintaining harmony with that spirit of divine love is no easy matter and demands conscious effort until and after it becomes firmly implanted in our nature. If it reigns within us, we become new creatures and new beings, especially if we were previously controlled by some evil spirit. Few of us are able to reach or remain on the highest possible plateau of Christ-like living but spiritual discipline and regular worship help us align and realign our total behavior with the Holy Spirit.

If we truly believe what we profess, praying for the Holy Spirit to be present is about like asking the sun to shine. There is no need or purpose for asking. God makes sure the Sun always shines because that is its nature. God's nature makes sure the Holy Spirit is always present and active, even if we did not ask for it and are unaware of its presence. Praying for its presence slaps God's face and possibly insinuates we control it. Even though we need never pray for its presence, we desperately need to pray that we become and remain keenly aware of its presence, power and purpose so that we may imitate its action where we are.

If our asking for it to be present is intended as a prayer for our increased awareness of and response to it, then let us rethink and rephrase that for which we ask and the way we ask for it.

Proof of the Holy Spirit's presence is not based on a stipulated or spectacular response from any person in whom it dwells. Some exuberant folk would have us believe it is present only if someone speaks in tongues, sways large crowds, accomplishes great miracles, performs uncommon feats, etc. Nothing can be further fromt he truth. The Holy Spirit is always present.

Spectacular occurrences are caused by various things and are no proof the Holy Spirit was responsible for what happened. If someone argues that it was, what do they say about Hitler, the Holocaust and Hiroshima? However, the Holy Spirit can and does accomplish great things.

Likewise, the minute size of an accomplishment is no guarantee the Holy Spirit is absent. It is active even in the ordinary events of every day living. That which we often call spectacular is nothing more than a compilation of the smaller things. The size of its accomplishment is relatively unimportant but the fact the Spirit is everywhere and anxious to intervene makes a tremendous difference. Furthermore, who among us is capable of distinguishing between the spectacular and the small? Nothing is small if it participates in imitating the action of God. Those who argue that the spectacular proves the Holy Spirit's presence may desire personal aggrandizement and may disregard one or more of the most fundamental principles pertaining to the Holy Spirit's presence.

Christian faith compels us to say some things are possible only through action of the Holy Spirit. God works in ways far beyond our limited human ability to recognize or understand. Since we lack complete understanding of how the Holy Spirit works, how can we make a definite declaration of what is or is not indicative of its presence and accomplishments? We can easily assign too little or too much credit to it. Evil intent and action sometimes produce good results. Is that the work of the Spirit, human ability or a combination of both? A Christian's "new birth" is a spectacular experience that would not happen without the work of the Spirit but would or could it happen without the person's conscious cooperation or the loving influence of another? Faithful effort from one who produces fruit of the Spirit is often instrumental in accomplishing divine purposes which may remain unknown to the one who put forth the effort. Would that have happened if the person had not deliberately and faithfully participated? Even as we attempt to affirm its presence, we always stand on shaky ground when we specifically state what is ori s not the work of the Spirit.

The Holy Spirit is not a special gift bestowed on those who are worthy of it, no matter how Christ-like we think we are, how hard we work, how financially successful we are or the number of degrees listed after our name. None of these things, or any combination of them, ever makes us worthy. The availability of the Holy Spirit does not depend on anything we may add. It always depends on God's gift to us. If at birth God implants his spirit in everyone, it makes no sense to say he later bestows it on those who, by doing something spectacular, make themselves worthy recipients. Sometime after birth, we may consciously choose to cooperate with God's spirit and be obedient to it but that still has nothing to do with our being worthy. Having done all within our power to imitate God's spirit and action, we remain unworthy on any basis other than his gift to everyone.

The Holy Spirit forever resides in us but we are responsible for enabling its growth and influence. We are not God's robots. No one knows precisely how that divinely implanted "seed" sprouts, matures, blossoms and produces fruit but apparently it does. Like other seed, it must have proper nourishment in a friendly environment before it grows or produces good fruit. If it becomes and remains a conscious part of our life, it will most likely be through our participation in a religious community, awareness of its availability, personal choice and religious discipline. An unassisted discovery or development of that part of our nature is extremely rare, if not impossible.

Even though we verbally deny the presence of the Holy Spirit in us and deliberately do what is less than good, that never takes away a fundamental part of who we are. We may demonstrate the presence of evil spirits in us to the degree that we and others think nothing holy remains. Even then, the essence of God implanted at birth remains, always ready to burst forth with new life and a new spirit if conditions for growth are present. Could it be that we do have some control over the Holy Spirit? Based on the above, the answer is both "no" and "yes." We have no control over its origin and existence. We cannot force it to do our bidding or cause it to do anything contrary to its nature and purpose.

At no point can we destroy God's spirit or force his hand. The ultimate dimensions of the Holy Spirit reach far beyond our control.

To some degree, we control its influence over us, and perhaps others. Apparently, God gave us the ability to choose what spirit dictates our behavior. That choice was originally hampered or helped by circumstance in early childhood, during our strong dependency on others. Persons are conduit through which evil or good spirits flow. In a sense, we not only have responsibility for ourselves but also for those under our tutelage and with whom we associate. A person's response to the Spirit tends to imitate those to whom they are tied, whether by birth, choice or circumstance. If we have a choice over a portion of what the Spirit does in and through us, if others affect our choice to cooperate with the Spirit and if we affect the choice of those around us, then we definitely have some control over the Spirit's activity as it seeks to act in and through us. If we continually refuse to recognize the Holy Spirit's tug on our heart, it is apparently willing to leave us where we are but it never gives up on us. A continuous refusal to respond to the Spirit's call will most likely have a negative effect on the rest of our life by limiting certain choices and producing unwanted results.

Though sometimes called by various names, God's active spirit existed prior to his creation of humanity and it will exist as long as he is God. His action and spirit are consistent and constant from the beginning. Biblical writers use imperfect human words to describe God's active spirit. They do not and cannot completely describe or define God's action but they forcefully affirm its constant presence.

The God of creation, Moses, Abraham, Isaac, Jacob, the prophets, Jesus, the disciples, Paul and the early Christians, is also our God who acts now as he did from the beginning. Having used numerous words, extensive space and extended time to convey thoughts and insights on the Holy Spirit, it remains beyond our ability to fully define, describe and understand. Hopefully, the extended process increased our desire to understand its nature and presence, thereby enabling us to think and speak honestly, openly and intelligently about it.

If the journey changed our concept of it from divine magic and bodiless heavenly beings to the recognition that it is the very nature of God, then our efforts were not in vain.

If we are more convinced the Holy Spirit sought from the first creation to the present to enlarge that divine spark given us at our own creation, we are wiser. If we have moved it from the exclusive realm of the divine and spectacular and discovered it is accessible to all and applicable in ordinary things, the journey was worthwhile. If we now believe that divine spirit should control us, we have a valid guide to evaluate what is a good or evil spirit in us. If we are convinced that the quality of our own life depends on our imitation of God's spirit, we are blessed.

CHAPTER TWELVE
A WISE WIDOW
Mark 12:41-44

41: And he sat down opposite the treasury, and watched the multitude putting money into the treasury. Many rich people put in large sums.

42: And a poor widow came, and put in two copper coins, which make a penny.

43: And he called his disciples to him, and said to them, "Truly, I say to you, this poor widow has put in more than all those who are contributing to the treasury.

44: For they all contributed out of their abundance; but she out of her poverty has put in everything she had, her whole living "

Mark's story about a poor widow is almost identical to the one found in Luke 21:1-4, but perhaps more provocative. It is another seemingly simple story easily categorized, if one is so inclined, as a "one-time event for a special person in a special place." For those who attach that label, it becomes another passage with little significance for our everyday experiences and another one of those "bible stories" easily discarded.

Could it be this short story is more than it first appears and contains fundamental truth applicable to all? People disregard this passage for numerous reasons. Some say the story is too simple and contains no profound truth so they seek religious guidance in more complicated and theologically laden passages. Others believe a poor widow could not teach anything to the rich, powerful and socially elite people around her. After all, she was very poor and they were very rich! Who should teach whom? Some consider her a foolish old woman who had lost all logical and practical skills required for self-preservation, especially if she was a beggar.

Other say she was a frail and failing old lady whose mind was overly saturated with religion, likely brainwashed by perverted priests in particular and by men in general.

If anyone wants an excuse to discard this story, any of the above will suffice. Judged strictly from a human perspective, these excuses just might contain a possible touch of truth. They apparently provide a possible and partial summation of the widow's physical conditions and situation. She is certainly on the lowest rung of the ladder to human success. If anyone expects God to reveal his truth only in spectacular and miraculous ways, this is not a spectacular story. If we refuse to look for God's revelations in the mundane and miserable events of human life, there is nothing further to be gained from pondering this passage.

However, judged from the perspective of Jesus, a prominent portion of the Gospel message is reflected in this short and simple story. Contrary to popular opinion, the mundane and miserable events of human life provide equal opportunities for God to reveal himself and his modus operandi. Could it be that is where he most often seeks our attention and response? Jesus used simple parables as a primary means to convey God's profound truth. It seems the simpler the parable, the more profound the truth. His great parables portray divine truth in mundane human existence. The prominent participants in those parables were most often ordinary people, events and conditions. Since Jesus used that type story to proclaim profound truth, the one about the widow has all the markings of something significant.

The story states no special reason why Jesus was in the temple courtyard. Apparently, his presence was nothing unusual. He may have been there for Sabbath worship. Like any devout Jewish male deeply involved in religious and secular events of his day, he naturally spent many hours there. From some unidentified source, Jesus acquired extensive and intricate knowledge about proper and improper religious activities conducted in and near the temple. The haughty, underhanded behavior of religious and civic leaders was well known to him.

Even though no records indicate it, he may have often spent time each day working or worshipping in and near the temple. Perhaps the words in Luke 21:1 suggest Jesus had just finished his meditation and prayers when "he looked up."

The unknown activities during Jesus' early adult life may have often positioned him in or near the temple. Could it be that he had a job or responsibility that necessitated his presence there? Perhaps he was a religious student or leader. That would readily explain how he acquired meticulous insight into daily life in and near the temple. When he became a teacher and public speaker, he took advantage of the opportunities offered by the temple community and used the temple's steps as the platform from which he spoke, as did other public speakers.

The temple area was the melting pot and the focal point of social and religious life for locals and visitors. An American practice and parallel may help us better understanding the temple's significance. Recall what we know about a multitude of America's rural communities in the not too distant past. Until recently, the church and the general merchandise store provided ideal places where people congregated to gossip, get the latest news and sometimes worship. These two places in particular were the social melting pot, the focal point that tied all of life together and gave it energy and excitement. People from near and far congregated in one or both to keep up with their friends, identify their enemies and get important news from beyond their little corner of the world. Issues were seriously debated and decided, sometimes by questionable means and for questionable ends. Adherence to customs and rules was emphasized and enforced. Politicians and prominent persons made sure they stopped by for a visit and a speech.

The impact and imprint of those two American places were in every way similar to the influence of the Jerusalem temple in Jesus' day. According to the story, it was a normal day in the temple court yard. People were engaged in routine matters. Jesus waited in or near the area where people regularly deposited their temple offerings.

Scholars tell us there were thirteen trumpet shaped metal receptacles specifically designed and located for the convenient collection of contributions. Each receptacle had a large open upper end that became progressively smaller as it funneled the coins downward into a designated treasure chest.

Each chest may have been labeled with a cause to which its content was dedicated. Their design and convenient placement resemble our modern-day unattended toll booths. The rich people ceremoniously paraded by the receptacles and made their contributions in a manner designed to impress bystanders with their offering, wealth and power. Their large coins made a loud noise as they clanged down the throat of the collecting devise. The size of their offering was indicated and announced by the noise it made and the number of times it was repeated. Could it be that the size, shape and material of those receptacles were not accidental?

While watching the normal activity of rich people contributing their coins, something suddenly caught the full attention of Jesus. The King James translation states it was "a certain poor widow" who stepped upon center stage. The RSV simply calls her "a poor widow." Could "a certain poor widow" be the better translation because it describes and identifies a well-known woman? Of all the poor widows in Jerusalem, was this one special, known by name and by her faithful daily contribution? Could it be that Jesus knew her name and financial condition, discovered at another time and place? In the temple courtyard, Jesus watched the rich make sure their large coins clanged loudly as they bounced off the metal and made their noisy journey, one after the other, to the collection box. The scene suddenly changed. It was as if the sea of rich and pompous people parted. The rich and famous stood on every side and in their midst stood a poor widow, extremely obvious by her clothing and demeanor. She made no attempt to hide her gift but she had no desire to call attention to it or herself. Perhaps she quietly slipped to the collection box and gave her gift, unknown and unnoticed by the rich. She knew the gift was small, compared to the gifts from the rich, but she also knew she wanted to make it.

The widow's gift made no loud noise as it quietly slithered down the throat of the metal receptacle. There was no attempt to make sure the next gift made more noticeable noise. She could not make a noisy contribution because she had only two small coins. They were the smallest Jewish coins in circulation, almost worthless as a medium of exchange and almost useless as noise makers in the collection device.

One's offering made a loud noise only if it was a large coin and she did not have one. Given the gist of the story, she would have given her last large coin if she had one.

Those two tiny coins were the total sum of her financial possessions. In her act of giving, Jesus saw what no temple priest, scribe or other bystander saw.

Jesus did not condemn the rich for withholding a portion of what they had. They needed something to live on. He faulted them for having improperly gained what they had, for failing to give the proper proportion and especially for the improper motive behind their giving. Had they properly gained their wealth and had the proper attitude or spirit about giving, their gifts would have also been vastly different. Jesus seems to insinuate that anything improperly gained cannot be purified by public and pompous giving to church and charity. No amount of material gifts ever purifies the spirit of the one who gives and one's inner spirit always dictates giving.

Jesus did not denounce the gifts of the rich to the temple treasury. We have no indication of his thought on the matter, other than his expressed opposition, here and on other occasions, to the purpose and manner in which they made them. Could it be that Jesus was making more than a simple statement when he said they "contributed out of their abundance?" It seems they had more than enough to meet their daily needs and wants. From the abundance they had, from their surplus over and above any immediate or anticipated need and desire, they gave only a small portion that did not in any way jeopardize their selfish lifestyle.

They likely gave to facilitate the acquisition of more wealth and power, not because they were persons of deep faith. For them, possessions were power and no person in his/her right mind would dare give away a large portion, let alone everything they had to live on.

Jesus saw things differently. Dollars don't count in measuring the true value of a person's gift. Genuine gifts are never measured by their size or monetary value but by what is left after giving. Gifts without cost actually count for little or nothing, especially in terms of religious matters, if not everywhere.

That is the gigantic contrast between the rich men and the poor widow. The gifts from the rich were motivated by pride and greed, costing almost nothing in proportion to what they had left. The widow's gift was motivated by a simple faith that encompassed everything she had. The size of each gift was not as important as the condition of the heart from which the gift came. Perhaps the widow knew a large gift given out of abundance never purifies it but a gift given from love is never too small to count.

Could it be that Jesus, in this passage and elsewhere, provides significant insight into proper Christian giving? The poor widow's faith and generosity deeply impressed Jesus and he used her as an object lesson to his disciples. Having recognized the significance of what he saw, he called his disciples and said something like, "Y'all come over here! Let me tell you what I just saw. That poor widow set the example for genuine giving." This biblical passage concludes by saying, "She put in everything she had, all she had to live on." Since Jesus was deeply impressed by the widow's gift, is he insinuating we should give everything we have to the church treasury? If so, most of us are in deep trouble. Is it possible Jesus actually meant something other than what the words first seem to say? Since Jesus used the words to emphasize a point, we must not take them lightly. If we accept those words exactly as they appear, if taken literally, their meaning is subject to serious misinterpretation.

Selfish, overly exuberant evangelists and uneducated preachers have a heyday with the statement, especially those who use all monetary gifts they receive as they wish and without accountability. For them, this passage provides religious leverage to elicit gifts from the uneducated, poor, aged and infirmed who desperately desire to give faithfully.

Selected bits of Bible verses quoted out of context, promises of punishment for those who refuse to support the designated person or cause, assurance of multiple blessings when they generously give and a few false tears result in unaffordable gifts from the uninformed faithful. Those who prey upon the poor, the aged and the infirm are identical to those in Jesus day who robbed the poor to increase their personal wealth.

Removing the overly exuberant and selfish fund raisers from the scene does not always correct the situation. Some faithful believers assume they must financially support every good cause that comes to their attention or they are not doing what God wants them to do.

Their number is relatively small and most of us have the opposite problem with giving! Convinced of the necessity to give, some deny basic personal needs in order to subsidize charitable and religious causes. They give not because some person presently puts pressure on them but because they lack adequate and proper religious insight. They are bound by and committed to a religious belief that may not be genuinely Christian, especially if any selfishness is attached to their gift. Contributions are saturated with selfishness when given to get more in return, given from fear of what will happeni f one does not give, given in order to maintain a reputation, or given to strictly follow a predetermined mathematical formula. Inquiring minds raise a pertinent point in response to the closing words of the story.

They honestly ask, "How can one literally give away all they have to live on," regardless of where it is given? If you have only two tiny and almost worthless coins, giving them away makes little difference in one's financial status.

If one has no daily responsibilities for others and no personal living expenses, like a homeless beggar woman, giving away everything you have changes almost nothing.

However, if one's wealth is measured in hundreds and thousands of dollars, much of which is already obligated to provide present and future needs for others and self, how can you literally give away all material possessions and survive? Speaking from a worldly perspective, we all know it cannot be done without serious repercussions. The widow could do that and survive but most of us cannot. Jesus no doubt knew that was impossible and impracticable for the average person and undoubtedly meant something other than a literal interpretation of his words.

Any who would be genuinely Christian cannot dismiss this as only a human interest story. If that is all it is, Jesus would not have highlighted the poor widow's gift. Is this another biblical passage where a literal interpretation of the written words robs it of its fundamental meaning? Could this be another biblical story deserving a new interpretation in order to understand its intended message? Is it another potent passage where we need not change the story, only our approach to and interpretation of it?

Could it be we often shun this passage because it forces us to consider what and why we give, or don't give? It gets to the heart of our religion, as well as our daily living and giving. Therefore, we may have little or no desire to deal with it or respond to it? This story strongly suggests that commitments are the basis for all behavior. Something or someone controls us. Our response to whatever controls us is rightfully described in religious terms. Our "god" controls us and our response to that control is worship, because we ascribe maximum worth to it. All our giving, if not all our living, is motivated either by trying to get something more in return or by giving what we have out of genuine gratitude andl ove. Jesus and the widow understood that. Misguided giving has masqueraded under the guise of Christian behavior for so long that we have serious difficulty knowing what is proper. It is no new issue.

Old Testament leaders specifically addressed proper giving and Jesus confronted it in his day. All religious leaders have not necessarily emphasized the proper motive for giving nor have they properly used gifts given to them. From the days of Adam to the present, some significant people, religiousl eaders and professing Christians were/ are more concerned with what they can get than with what they can give. Under the banner of genuine religion, they have created serious difficulties by misleading others.

A closer look at this story will help us better understand Christian giving. If nothing else, this story reflects a woman who lived by faith and gratitude. She basically had no material possessions and she knew it. What she possessed was of little use to her but she knew where it would make a big difference, if not in the offering box then in her life of faith. It seems she gladly gave it without any pressure to do so or any promise of more in return. Even though she had almost no material possessions, she had faith that her future material needs would be met from some unidentified source. We have no knowledge of her thoughts but her willingness to freely give reflects her faith and the genuine Christian spirit. Jesus used her to emphasize a fundamental lesson about giving material possessions. They are always measured in proportion to what is left after giving. The widow gave only a minute gift but it was one hundred per cent of what she had to give. In contrast, the rich contributors gave much larger monetary gifts, but only a minute portions of their surplus. After their gifts, the rich still had almost as much as before. When Jesus said the widow had given more than all the rest, he did not mean the monetary value of her gift exceeded the total sum given by the rich. A literal interpretation of his words argues the impossible, makes absolutely no sense, and misses the whole point of the story.

Obviously, Jesus meant what the words do not literally say. In proportion to what she had to give, or had left after giving, she gave far more than the rich.

Jesus never said, here or elsewhere, one should give away all of their material possessions to the church or charity. He undoubtedly understood the impracticality and impossibility of such action. Proportionate giving appears to be the key element that captured Jesus' attention and apparently is what he requires of his followers. Here is our problem because we have a tough time deciding precisely what proportionate giving means and how to do it.

As indicated earlier, that problem is not new. Ancient Israel required faithful followers to give a tithe as their offering, sometimes taken from unidentified substances and sometimes from the "first fruit" of their labors and flock. We lack specific information on the precise application of this requirement but it seems to have been an imperfect solution. Based on biblical admonitions and ancient practices, numerous Christians of our day believe tithing is the proper approach for proportionate giving. That is an excellent place to start but is does not resolve our problem.

A tithe is commonly considered one tenth of something. Astute minds immediately ask, "One tenth of what?" Previous religious instructions and present insight largely determine our personal answer. Preachers, parents and fellow parishioners must have their personal answer but their answer is not necessarily mine.

Where do we begin to calculate our tithe? Is it a tenth of our total income, regardless of our present situation? What about the money we saved on the vegetables we grew in our garden or the calf we raised, butchered and put in the deep freeze? Is a modern widow required to give one tenth of her paltry social security check and do without food, medicine and utilities?

Is a tithe calculated on what is left after all living expenses are paid, even if some of us live extravagantly? If so, we can easily escape the requirement to tithe by adopting a lifestyle that requires expenditure of all our income, no matter how large or how little. If we have luxury items like extra cars, a large boat, swimming pool, summer vacation, etc., where do we draw the line between necessity and luxury? What about the ill, poor, unemployed, underpaid, etc.?

Are they expected to give a tithe of whatever they get, regardless of the extra burden it places on their already inadequate income? Does tithing include a second job for which we get paid in cash with no report sent to the IRS? How do we handle unexpected gifts, inheritance and profits from the sale of items originally purchased with money left after our tithe? It becomes immediately apparent that we have no adequate solution that fits every situation and condition confronted by devoutly religious people.

Tithing may first appear practical but it is problematic. A designated and known starting point for calculating a stipulated percentage of "something" would make proportionate giving measurable and simpler. It would also make it legalistic, not faithful stewardship. It would facilitate easy judgment of any who failed to meet the imposed standard, regardless of the unknown circumstances under which they exist. It might easily become the litmus test, the single standard, by which another person's Christian faith is judged. It would cause unavoidable pain for deeply religious persons who have few material possessions.

When someone asks the meaning of proportionate giving, "tithe" is an inadequate answer for many reasons. First, it is almost impossible to identify a specific or logical starting point. Second, it is based solely on a legalistic requirement that demands only a certain percent of one's material possessions, regardless of how large or how small. Third, it allows for human manipulation designed to appease one's conscience by using shady mathematical calculations. Fourth, it is most often applied only to material possessions. Fifth, it has little or no connection to a life of faith and gratitude. Sixth, it sounds as if God wants only one tenth of something and the other ninety percent is of no concern to him.

A partial solution to our dilemma comes from the simple story of the widow's gift. Could it be that we have once more completely overlooked the profound significance of a simple statement by Jesus? The NRSV translates the closing words of Mark 12:44, "She put in everything she had, all she had to live on."

Could it be that the statement needs one added word that may have been implied by or was a part of the original text? What if it really says she "put in everything she had 'including' all she had to live on ?"

Notice the distinct difference between the two. We can give "all we have to live on," i.e., primarily our material possessions, without giving "all we have," i.e., material possessions and everything beyond. This interpretation indicates Jesus identified two distinct types of giving. One type is limited strictly to the material and the second type includes the material and all else. Giving only "all we have to live on" (the material) without giving "all we have" (the non- material and material) may be as detrimental to us as not giving anything. Giving only what we have to live on is a legalistic approach to religion but giving to God all we have is a response of faith.

From the Christian perspective, proportionate giving requires one hundred percent of "all we have!" Jesus and the poor widow knew that. God is not pleased or appeased with a measly ten percent of something. He is not pleased with fifty, seventy-five or even ninety percent. Like the poor widow, genuine Christian giving requires all we have which includes all we have to live on. God accepts one hundred percent of all we have at our disposal or he accepts nothing.

This concept is radically different from what most of us were taught in Sunday school and sermons. To our detriment, we heard much more about tithing than about stewardship. That is odd because the New Testament addresses the proper use of possessions almost exclusively under the subject of stewardship, not tithing. Due to what we were taught long ago, some of us may have difficulty accepting the fact that stewardship is more important than tithing. Proportionate giving focuses primarily on faithful stewardship and has only a secondary concern for tithing.

Numerous New Testament stories speak specifically about stewardship but we need not discuss them here. A good insight into proportionate giving is found in II Timothy 2:15 (KJV) where Christians are encouraged to "rightly divide the word of truth."

In reference to proportionate giving, that author might also admonish us to "rightfully divide all we have." A distinctive mark of Christians is their declaration that God owns everything.

With genuine gratitude in their hearts, they purposely and joyfully commit themselves to be faithful stewards of that with which they have been entrusted. However, a declaration to be a faithful steward is only the first step in resolving the problem of proportionate giving. Grateful acknowledgement to whom everything belongs does not remove personal responsibility for proper management of everything entrusted to our care, material or otherwise. God is not going to do for us what he expects us to do. He will not manage it for us. Good stewardship demands responsible action and all our actions indicate the kind of stewards we really are.

By definition, Christian stewardship is never practiced in order to get something in return. Any positive results and rewards received from practicing it are byproducts and not the reason for it. It is practiced out of gratitude for what God has already given us, and nothing more! Otherwise, it becomes selfish and negates the Christian concept of faithful stewardship. The poor widow knew that but it is extremely difficult for many professing Christians to accept it.

Could it be the poor widow provides precise guidance which we often disregard? She gave everything she had. She acted on faith, not by the rules of her world or by the examples of unscrupulous religious leaders. No one can live as she unless they first give everything they have to God. For a life based on genuine faith, dollars don't count, at least as the starting point for stewardship. A life motivated by genuine faith in God accepts the necessity to be a faithful steward and then acts accordingly in every situation. Genuine Christian faith does not demand a simple or exact set of answers to the questions on proportionate giving. There are none, regardless of our desire for them or our repeated attempt to create them. As difficult as it may seem, we are responsible for our stewardship in our unique situation and under every condition. No set of specific rules applies to everyone.

Technically speaking, Christian stewards, like the widow, actually have nothing left to claim as their own. That is their only rule. They are managers, not owners, because they have given everything to God. They are only stewards over that entrusted to their management. Therefore, when Christians speak of what they have, they must always mean that over which they have management responsibilities and not that which they personally possess. Any selfish claim of ownership negates proper stewardship!

This fundamental principle of "stewardship instead of ownership" is absolutely essential for all Christians. Secular society argues the opposite by emphasizing ownership. The rich people in Jesus' story about the poor widow perfectly illustrate many modern beliefs and practices. In many ways and for many reasons, Christians are constantly tempted to believe society and to boast of what they personally possess. The matter gets more complicated when Christians must primarily use the language of secular society to speak about stewardship. Some words used by Christians sound the same but they must reflect a different meaning from what society gives them. Therefore, Christians must exercise extreme caution when speaking of what they have. Extra effort is necessary so that others know a Christian's implied ownership always mean that for which they have stewardship responsibility. Behavior always speaks louder than words!

Any selfish claim to ownership, either from disbelief or refusal to follow the principle, prompts our wrestling with the issue of tithing and how much we should give to God. Full acceptance of the stewardship principle gives no absolute guide for proportional giving but it does put us in the proper position to make appropriate decisions. Since we constantly swim against the secular tide, reminders that we are only stewards are helpful, if not necessary. Could it be the widow gave her only two coins as a vivid reminder that she really had nothing other than faith? Did Jesus tell this story because he also wanted us to know that?

Could it be that God does not really care how or where we exercise our stewardship, as long as it supports his will and his way? If that is true, it revolutionizes much of what we were taught and sets us free to be good stewards. It reemphasizes the necessity for careful and proper stewardship but enables us to be less anxious about its precise distribution. Perhaps there is no predetermined amount or worthwhile cause to which we should give, as long as we are God's good stewards with everything at our disposal.

Proper stewardship is not haphazard or accidental but its specific application is somewhat different for everyone. We are more likely to exercise proper stewardship after intellectually considering the seriousness of a need, our ability to meet the need, a personal preference, and leadership of The Spirit. The plethora of places needing and deserving our support provides greater responsibility and more opportunities for wise choices.

Giving one hundred percent to God does not necessarily mean giving one hundred percent of all we have to the church or charity. That is not the point Jesus made in the story about the poor and faithful widow. If it were even possible, doing that would rob the rest of life of its meaning and purpose. It would indicate nothing else matters to God. Such nonsense is unacceptable because everything connected to human life matters to God. Even though church and charity are high on the priority list, they take their place among all the other important necessities.

Proper stewardship encompasses a personal allowance for food, clothing and shelter. God designed health and happiness as a natural and necessary part of our existence. Basic essentials are necessary for further stewardship. Proper care of self is also care for one of God's creatures. There is no way to maintain a meaningful life without using a portion of our material possessions for self-preservation. Even though our effort to maintain a quality life is apparently ordained by God, it must never be most important to us. If so, that is idolatry.

Christians must seriously consider proper use of one hundred percent of what they have, not just ten percent of some unidentifiable amount. As we practice good stewardship, we must seriously and deliberately consider more than the size of our contributions to the church and charity. We must also consider the size, location and cost of our house; the number, make, price and age of the automobiles we drive; the expense, frequency and results of leisure activities; the treatment of our body and the bodies of others; the protection of the environment; the place, time and manner of worship; the efforts to eradicate evil, poverty, and ignorance; the amount of time, talents and possessions we give to others; etc. That kind of stewardship is never based exclusively on what we have but it is always based on what we have already given to God. It comes from a realization that we gave up our claim to anything so that we may purposely and properly use everything God entrusted to our management.

Since proper stewardship requires careful management, we must manage not only the expensive items but also inexpensive ones; not only the thousands of dollars but also the pennies and nickels; not only the months and years but also the hours and minutes; not only the professional talents but also the everyday opportunities to show kindness, mercy and love. Christian stewardship of all we have requires constant application and is a full-time job.

Good stewardship naturally includes gifts to church and charity but how do we determine our appropriate giving to them? Even though some people make a sharp distinction between these two, the New Testament seldom separates them. Most often, Jesus seemed more concerned about providing charity than about temple offerings. However, at no point did Jesus deny the necessity for temple offerings. Whether we take them separately or together, a crucial issue is always the appropriate amount of time, talent and treasure to give.

Good stewardship that includes appropriate giving to the church and charity does not just happen. God does not participate with our bank in his pre-approved and predetermined automatic withdrawal system.

Gifts to church and charity are carefully planned, proportionate, and only occasionally spasmodic. They are timely, not whenever we think about it or whenever it is convenient or whenever our conscious bothers us or when someone puts an unavoidable squeeze on us.

It is most helpful, perhaps necessary, for us to prayerfully and thoughtfully consider what we will probably have during a designated period. Additionally, seriously consider all the things we want to support and how to rightfully divide what we have. Having done that, make a pledge (budget) covering our estimated and intended expenditure for each item or area, including living expenses. Our announced estimated gift to our church or a charitable organization is a deliberate act of faith on our part and extremely helpful for those who budget the expenditure of such gifts. Deliberate and designated giving enables better stewardship. Following this procedure may not drastically change the amount we contribute to our church or charity but it usually means we reach our decision through a new process, especially when we concentrate more on stewardship than on tithing. It allows support of all worthwhile causes and gives freedom for the aged, ill andi mpoverished to spend on themselves most of what they have to live on without guilt.

Proper stewardship also demands deliberate and designated giving of time and talents. Even though somewhat different from material matters, they deserve and require specific attention from proper stewards because they are just as important as material possessions. An emphasis only on tithing disregards a large portion of proper stewardship. At some point and in some manner, we all have time and talents to promote God's will and way. Much of what was said about material possessions, with only minor adjustments, is applicable to proper stewardship of time and talents.

Proper stewardship includes proportionate giving to the church and charity… if and when one is able to give! Proportional giving must also include conditional giving.

Persons with little or no material possessions are often exempt in a discussion on stewardship. Faithful stewardship is required of every Christian. We all have something to manage and give. If low income, poor health, high cost of housing and food, etc., leave one financially drained, she/he need not further deprive themselves by giving a portion of their income to others. When unavoidable, it is not unchristian, just religiously uncomfortable, for one to spend their entire income on the basic necessities of life. It could be unchristian i f one fails to meet basic human needs because they gave too much money to church and charity. Having no material gifts to share should cause no guilt because there are other things to give. Some have far more free time or talent than money. What they have to give is worth more than money can buy. They deserve and need an opportunity to give it because that is "what they have." What does proportionate giving require from each of us? The first answer is one hundred percent of everything, as previously stated. How we divide it is another matter. It is very interesting to note we repeatedly return to that question in search of a specific and measurable answer for distributing our material possessions. Could it be we continually burden ourselves frantically searching for a satisfactory answer to an incorrect and improper question? Could that search be unchristian behavior? Being interpreted, the question sounds as if we keep asking, "How much am I required to give away in order to be Christian?" The Christian's question is not "How much do I have to give away to prove I am a Christian?" It is, "How can I most effectively serve God with one hundred percent of everything he entrusted to my management?" That latter question turns our secular world upside down and may even dismantle certain teachings that were once called Christian.

The secular world and some so called religious folk often ask, "What can I get and how much can I rightfully keep?" The Christian question concerns itself with how to make best use of everything over which we are stewards. As indicated in the last verse of the biblical passage under consideration, Jesus knew one does not and cannot properly address the matter of faithful stewardship until they have gratefully and gladly given all they have to God.

As Christians, how can we best serve God after recognizing we are nothing more than stewards over what he trusted to our management? Finding the proper answer to this question is most difficult but absolutely necessary. The emphasis shifts from the amount we must give to the most effective use of everything under our management, including time, talents, material possessions, intellect, etc., all of which we should have already given to God. Any answer for how we rightfully distribute that and how we may best serve God can be only a general guideline for individual application when and where appropriate. This is a personal matter for every faithful steward.

If we live as good stewards, there seems to be one fundamental principle under-girding all else. Our life will constantly reflect a Christ-like, generous and unselfish spirit, always open to the needs of others and ourselves. Can we be truly Christian otherwise? Assisted by prayer, meditation and intellect, we focus on needs and our ability to meet them, whether ours or another's. At one point, a neighbor may need financial help but on another occasion, they may have greater need for a kind and encouraging word or a helping hand so they may help themselves. Sometimes we may be able to meet their physical and financial needs but at other times we may have nothing more than genuine concern for them. Could it be others first need to know our genuine concern? If we are what we claim to be, we can at least provide that and they will have been truly helped. We then move beyond that point as their needs and our abilities meet.

Good stewardship does not deny that which enables personal health, happiness and wholeness. We take those things seriously so that we may remain faithful stewards. We must never forget our own importance but we must never usurp God's place in the created order.

God surely does not demand everyone be a pauper, hermit or beggar. He expects us to properly care for ourselves, when and where possible. Comfortable homes, delicious food, nice clothing, advanced education, new automobiles, etc. are not denied but they must be deliberately balanced between enough and too much.

There are no set rules which guarantee living at the level between "enough" and "too much." Human conditions and experiences in our everyday secular world encourage our quest for a guarantee. Life in the secular world encourages the establishment of specific percentages, formulas, and exact rules for giving. Some professing Christians erroneously believe they have that exact formula. Genuine stewardship is the only fixed rule and negates the need for any other. If we could formulate a fixed rule on where, when and what to give to church, charity and elsewhere, it would soon come "unfixed." Situations and conditions constantly change and the rule would be obsolete and incomplete. Our relationship to God is far more important than fixed rules. The poor widow no doubt knew that. Jesus also knew it.

Could there be at least one more partially hidden jewel in Jesus' story about the poor widow? Her willingness to give away all she had may indicate she knew something many of us do not. If many of us know it, we refuse to follow it. Could it be that we keep some things in reversed proportion to which they are given away? Try to keep them and they disappear but give them away and we have even more. It is impossible to keep many of them unless we repeatedly and unselfishly give them away. They only provide lasting benefit for others and us when shared. That is especially true for certain talents and behavior patterns. Talents soon die when hoarded but multiply when given away. In a sense, similar things may be said about the use of our time and possessions. They also seem to vanish without a trace unless carefully and prayerfully dispensed. Perhaps the poor widow knew that.

A poor widow gladly gave two tiny coins for her temple offering. She had no idea a simple demonstration of her faith would make such an impact on Jesus. For him, her action illustrated one hundred percent giving.

She gave all she had to live on only because she had previously given all she had to God. This is not a one-time special event for special people under special conditions. It is an illustration of genuine stewardship. Could it be we must imitate her in order to be genuinely Christian?

JOSEPH C. WAY

Printed in the USA
CPSIA information can be obtained
at www.ICGtesting.com
LVHW050740171223
766490LV00098B/3693